C000052851

Investment Priorities
Complete Self-Assessment Guide

The guidance in this Self-Assessment is based on Investment Priorities best practices and standards in business process architecture, design and quality management. The guidance is also based on the professional judgment of the individual collaborators listed in the Acknowledgments.

Notice of rights

Trademarks

Table of Contents

About The Art of Service

The Art of Service, Business Process Architects since 2000, is dedicated to helping stakeholders achieve excellence.

Defining, designing, creating, and implementing a process to solve a stakeholders challenge or meet an objective is the most valuable role… In EVERY group, company, organization and department.

Unless you're talking a one-time, single-use project, there should be a process. Whether that process is managed and implemented by humans, AI, or a combination of the two, it needs to be designed by someone with a complex enough perspective to ask the right questions.

Someone capable of asking the right questions and step back and say, 'What are we really trying to accomplish here? And is there a different way to look at it?'

With The Art of Service's Standard Requirements Self-Assessments, we empower people who can do just that — whether their title is marketer, entrepreneur, manager, salesperson, consultant, Business Process Manager, executive assistant, IT Manager, CIO etc... —they are the people who rule the future. They are people who watch the process as it happens, and ask the right questions to make the process work better.

Contact us when you need any support with this Self-Assessment and any help with templates, blue-prints and examples of standard documents you might need:

http://theartofservice.com
service@theartofservice.com

Included Resources - how to access

Included with your purchase of the book is the Investment

Priorities Self-Assessment Spreadsheet Dashboard which contains all questions and Self-Assessment areas and auto-generates insights, graphs, and project RACI planning - all with examples to get you started right away.

How? Simply send an email to
access@theartofservice.com
with this books' title in the subject to get the Investment Priorities Self Assessment Tool right away.

You will receive the following contents with New and Updated specific criteria:

- The latest quick edition of the book in PDF

- The latest complete edition of the book in PDF, which criteria correspond to the criteria in...

- The Self-Assessment Excel Dashboard, and...

- Example pre-filled Self-Assessment Excel Dashboard to get familiar with results generation

- In-depth specific Checklists covering the topic

- Project management checklists and templates to assist with implementation

INCLUDES LIFETIME SELF ASSESSMENT UPDATES

Every self assessment comes with Lifetime Updates and Lifetime Free Updated Books. Lifetime Updates is an industry-first feature which allows you to receive verified self assessment updates, ensuring you always have the most accurate information at your fingertips.

Get it now- you will be glad you did - do it now, before you forget.

Send an email to **access@theartofservice.com** with this books' title in the subject to get the Investment Priorities Self Assessment Tool right away.

Purpose of this Self-Assessment

This Self-Assessment has been developed to improve understanding of the requirements and elements of Investment Priorities, based on best practices and standards in business process architecture, design and quality management.

It is designed to allow for a rapid Self-Assessment to determine how closely existing management practices and procedures correspond to the elements of the Self-Assessment.

The criteria of requirements and elements of Investment Priorities have been rephrased in the format of a Self-Assessment questionnaire, with a seven-criterion scoring system, as explained in this document.

In this format, even with limited background knowledge of Investment Priorities, a manager can quickly review existing operations to determine how they measure up to the standards. This in turn can serve as the starting point of a 'gap analysis' to identify management tools or system elements that might usefully be implemented in the organization to help improve overall performance.

How to use the Self-Assessment

On the following pages are a series of questions to identify to what extent your Investment Priorities initiative is complete in comparison to the requirements set in standards.

To facilitate answering the questions, there is a space in front of each question to enter a score on a scale of '1' to '5'.

1 Strongly Disagree

2 Disagree

3 Neutral

4 Agree

5 Strongly Agree

Read the question and rate it with the following in front of mind:

'In my belief,
the answer to this question is clearly defined'.

There are two ways in which you can choose to interpret this statement;
1. how aware are you that the answer to the question is clearly defined
2. for more in-depth analysis you can choose to gather evidence and confirm the answer to the question. This obviously will take more time, most Self-Assessment users opt for the first way to interpret the question and dig deeper later on based on the outcome of the overall Self-Assessment.

A score of '1' would mean that the answer is not clear at all, where a '5' would mean the answer is crystal clear and defined. Leave emtpy when the question is not applicable or you don't want to answer it, you can skip it without affecting your score. Write your score in the space provided.

After you have responded to all the appropriate statements in each section, compute your average score for that section, using the formula provided, and round to the nearest tenth. Then transfer to the corresponding spoke in the Investment Priorities Scorecard on the second next page of the Self-Assessment.

Your completed Investment Priorities Scorecard will give you a clear presentation of which Investment Priorities areas need attention.

Investment Priorities
Scorecard Example

Example of how the finalized Scorecard can look like:

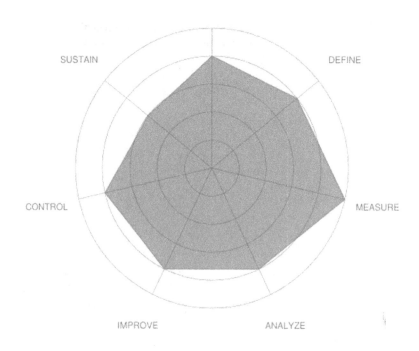

Investment Priorities
Scorecard

Your Scores:

BEGINNING OF THE SELF-ASSESSMENT:

CRITERION #1: RECOGNIZE

INTENT: Be aware of the need for change. Recognize that there is an unfavorable variation, problem or symptom.

In my belief, the answer to this question is clearly defined:

5 Strongly Agree

4 Agree

3 Neutral

2 Disagree

1 Strongly Disagree

1. For your investment priorities project, identify and describe the business environment, is there more than one layer to the business environment?
<--- Score

2. Is it clear when you think of the day ahead of you what activities and tasks you need to complete?
<--- Score

3. Are there any specific expectations or concerns about the investment priorities team, investment priorities itself?
<--- Score

4. What extra resources will you need?
<--- Score

5. Consider your own investment priorities project, what types of organizational problems do you think might be causing or affecting your problem, based on the work done so far?
<--- Score

6. Are there any revenue recognition issues?
<--- Score

7. What prevents you from making the changes you know will make you a more effective investment priorities leader?
<--- Score

8. Did you miss any major investment priorities issues?
<--- Score

9. Have you identified your investment priorities key performance indicators?
<--- Score

10. What would happen if investment priorities weren't done?
<--- Score

11. Do you have/need 24-hour access to key personnel?
<--- Score

12. To what extent does each concerned units management team recognize investment priorities as an effective investment?
<--- Score

13. Are employees recognized for desired behaviors?
<--- Score

14. What activities does the governance board need to consider?
<--- Score

15. How can auditing be a preventative security measure?
<--- Score

16. Are losses recognized in a timely manner?
<--- Score

17. Is it needed?
<--- Score

18. Whom do you really need or want to serve?
<--- Score

19. How are you going to measure success?
<--- Score

20. How are the investment priorities's objectives aligned to the group's overall stakeholder strategy?
<--- Score

21. What situation(s) led to this investment priorities Self Assessment?
<--- Score

22. Is the quality assurance team identified?
<--- Score

23. What is the recognized need?
<--- Score

24. Will a response program recognize when a crisis occurs and provide some level of response?
<--- Score

25. Where do you need to exercise leadership?
<--- Score

26. Are problem definition and motivation clearly presented?
<--- Score

27. To what extent would your organization benefit from being recognized as a award recipient?
<--- Score

28. Think about the people you identified for your investment priorities project and the project responsibilities you would assign to them, what kind of training do you think they would need to perform these responsibilities effectively?
<--- Score

29. Why is this needed?
<--- Score

30. Who defines the rules in relation to any given issue?
<--- Score

31. What training and capacity building actions are needed to implement proposed reforms?
<--- Score

32. Are there investment priorities problems defined?
<--- Score

33. What do you need to start doing?
<--- Score

34. How do you take a forward-looking perspective in identifying investment priorities research related to market response and models?
<--- Score

35. How do you identify subcontractor relationships?
<--- Score

36. Do you know what you need to know about investment priorities?
<--- Score

37. How does it fit into your organizational needs and tasks?
<--- Score

38. Are there recognized investment priorities problems?
<--- Score

39. How do you assess your investment priorities workforce capability and capacity needs, including skills, competencies, and staffing levels?
<--- Score

40. What is the problem or issue?

<--- Score

41. How do you identify the kinds of information that you will need?
<--- Score

42. What needs to stay?
<--- Score

43. What vendors make products that address the investment priorities needs?
<--- Score

44. What resources or support might you need?
<--- Score

45. Does your organization need more investment priorities education?
<--- Score

46. What creative shifts do you need to take?
<--- Score

47. What are the minority interests and what amount of minority interests can be recognized?
<--- Score

48. Can management personnel recognize the monetary benefit of investment priorities?
<--- Score

49. What investment priorities coordination do you need?
<--- Score

50. How are training requirements identified?

<--- Score

51. What tools and technologies are needed for a custom investment priorities project?
<--- Score

52. How do you recognize an objection?
<--- Score

53. Are controls defined to recognize and contain problems?
<--- Score

54. Who needs to know about investment priorities?
<--- Score

55. How do you recognize an investment priorities objection?
<--- Score

56. What problems are you facing and how do you consider investment priorities will circumvent those obstacles?
<--- Score

57. What are the timeframes required to resolve each of the issues/problems?
<--- Score

58. As a sponsor, customer or management, how important is it to meet goals, objectives?
<--- Score

59. Who needs to know?
<--- Score

60. Are there regulatory / compliance issues?
<--- Score

61. Who needs what information?
<--- Score

62. What are your needs in relation to investment priorities skills, labor, equipment, and markets?
<--- Score

63. How much are sponsors, customers, partners, stakeholders involved in investment priorities? In other words, what are the risks, if investment priorities does not deliver successfully?
<--- Score

64. Who needs budgets?
<--- Score

65. What are the expected benefits of investment priorities to the stakeholder?
<--- Score

66. Does investment priorities create potential expectations in other areas that need to be recognized and considered?
<--- Score

67. What is the extent or complexity of the investment priorities problem?
<--- Score

68. What investment priorities events should you attend?
<--- Score

69. What does investment priorities success mean to the stakeholders?
<--- Score

70. What should be considered when identifying available resources, constraints, and deadlines?
<--- Score

71. Why the need?
<--- Score

72. Where is training needed?
<--- Score

73. Do you recognize investment priorities achievements?
<--- Score

74. Will new equipment/products be required to facilitate investment priorities delivery, for example is new software needed?
<--- Score

75. Who else hopes to benefit from it?
<--- Score

76. Do you need different information or graphics?
<--- Score

77. Which needs are not included or involved?
<--- Score

78. Are your goals realistic? Do you need to redefine your problem? Perhaps the problem has changed or maybe you have reached your goal and need to set a new one?

<--- Score

79. Which issues are too important to ignore?
<--- Score

80. What investment priorities capabilities do you need?
<--- Score

81. When a investment priorities manager recognizes a problem, what options are available?
<--- Score

82. Looking at each person individually – does every one have the qualities which are needed to work in this group?
<--- Score

83. Does the problem have ethical dimensions?
<--- Score

84. What are the stakeholder objectives to be achieved with investment priorities?
<--- Score

85. Would you recognize a threat from the inside?
<--- Score

86. Is the need for organizational change recognized?
<--- Score

87. Who are your key stakeholders who need to sign off?
<--- Score

88. What is the smallest subset of the problem you

can usefully solve?
<--- Score

89. What do employees need in the short term?
<--- Score

90. What are the investment priorities resources needed?
<--- Score

91. Will it solve real problems?
<--- Score

92. What is the investment priorities problem definition? What do you need to resolve?
<--- Score

93. Are employees recognized or rewarded for performance that demonstrates the highest levels of integrity?
<--- Score

94. Do you need to avoid or amend any investment priorities activities?
<--- Score

95. What needs to be done?
<--- Score

96. What investment priorities problem should be solved?
<--- Score

97. Are you dealing with any of the same issues today as yesterday? What can you do about this?
<--- Score

98. Will investment priorities deliverables need to be tested and, if so, by whom?
<--- Score

99. What information do users need?
<--- Score

Add up total points for this section:
_ _ _ _ _ = Total points for this section

Divided by: _ _ _ _ _ _ (number of statements answered) = _ _ _ _ _ _
Average score for this section

Transfer your score to the investment priorities Index at the beginning of the Self-Assessment.

CRITERION #2: DEFINE:

INTENT: Formulate the stakeholder problem. Define the problem, needs and objectives.

In my belief, the answer to this question is clearly defined:

5 Strongly Agree

4 Agree

3 Neutral

2 Disagree

1 Strongly Disagree

1. Have the customer needs been translated into specific, measurable requirements? How?
<--- Score

2. What is a worst-case scenario for losses?
<--- Score

3. Has anyone else (internal or external to the group) attempted to solve this problem or a similar one

before? If so, what knowledge can be leveraged from these previous efforts?
<--- Score

4. How was the 'as is' process map developed, reviewed, verified and validated?
<--- Score

5. Who approved the investment priorities scope?
<--- Score

6. What key stakeholder process output measure(s) does investment priorities leverage and how?
<--- Score

7. Where can you gather more information?
<--- Score

8. How will the investment priorities team and the group measure complete success of investment priorities?
<--- Score

9. What information do you gather?
<--- Score

10. Do you have organizational privacy requirements?
<--- Score

11. What are the requirements for audit information?
<--- Score

12. Is the team adequately staffed with the desired cross-functionality? If not, what additional resources are available to the team?
<--- Score

13. Is there any additional investment priorities definition of success?
<--- Score

14. In what way can you redefine the criteria of choice clients have in your category in your favor?
<--- Score

15. Have all basic functions of investment priorities been defined?
<--- Score

16. What is the scope of investment priorities?
<--- Score

17. What are the boundaries of the scope? What is in bounds and what is not? What is the start point? What is the stop point?
<--- Score

18. When is/was the investment priorities start date?
<--- Score

19. Will a investment priorities production readiness review be required?
<--- Score

20. Is special investment priorities user knowledge required?
<--- Score

21. Has the investment priorities work been fairly and/or equitably divided and delegated among team members who are qualified and capable to perform the work? Has everyone contributed?

<--- Score

22. What constraints exist that might impact the team?
<--- Score

23. Have all of the relationships been defined properly?
<--- Score

24. What is out of scope?
<--- Score

25. What is the definition of investment priorities excellence?
<--- Score

26. Is investment priorities linked to key stakeholder goals and objectives?
<--- Score

27. Who is gathering information?
<--- Score

28. How can the value of investment priorities be defined?
<--- Score

29. What are the dynamics of the communication plan?
<--- Score

30. Is the investment priorities scope manageable?
<--- Score

31. Is there a critical path to deliver investment

priorities results?
<--- Score

32. What intelligence can you gather?
<--- Score

33. How do you keep key subject matter experts in the loop?
<--- Score

34. How do you gather requirements?
<--- Score

35. When are meeting minutes sent out? Who is on the distribution list?
<--- Score

36. Is the improvement team aware of the different versions of a process: what they think it is vs. what it actually is vs. what it should be vs. what it could be?
<--- Score

37. What gets examined?
<--- Score

38. How do you build the right business case?
<--- Score

39. What are the compelling stakeholder reasons for embarking on investment priorities?
<--- Score

40. Are required metrics defined, what are they?
<--- Score

41. Is the scope of investment priorities defined?

<--- Score

42. Are different versions of process maps needed to account for the different types of inputs?
<--- Score

43. When is the estimated completion date?
<--- Score

44. What is the worst case scenario?
<--- Score

45. What knowledge or experience is required?
<--- Score

46. Is investment priorities required?
<--- Score

47. What baselines are required to be defined and managed?
<--- Score

48. How do you gather investment priorities requirements?
<--- Score

49. How do you catch investment priorities definition inconsistencies?
<--- Score

50. How do you gather the stories?
<--- Score

51. What information should you gather?
<--- Score

52. Has a project plan, Gantt chart, or similar been developed/completed?

<--- Score

53. What are the Roles and Responsibilities for each team member and its leadership? Where is this documented?

<--- Score

54. Has the improvement team collected the 'voice of the customer' (obtained feedback – qualitative and quantitative)?

<--- Score

55. Is the work to date meeting requirements?

<--- Score

56. How would you define investment priorities leadership?

<--- Score

57. What are (control) requirements for investment priorities Information?

<--- Score

58. What are the investment priorities tasks and definitions?

<--- Score

59. Scope of sensitive information?

<--- Score

60. Are the investment priorities requirements complete?

<--- Score

61. How did the investment priorities manager receive input to the development of a investment priorities improvement plan and the estimated completion dates/times of each activity?
<--- Score

62. What specifically is the problem? Where does it occur? When does it occur? What is its extent?
<--- Score

63. Has your scope been defined?
<--- Score

64. Has a team charter been developed and communicated?
<--- Score

65. Are there any constraints known that bear on the ability to perform investment priorities work? How is the team addressing them?
<--- Score

66. What happens if investment priorities's scope changes?
<--- Score

67. What customer feedback methods were used to solicit their input?
<--- Score

68. Does the team have regular meetings?
<--- Score

69. Is there regularly 100% attendance at the team meetings? If not, have appointed substitutes attended to preserve cross-functionality and full

representation?
<--- Score

70. What is the scope of the investment priorities effort?
<--- Score

71. What investment priorities services do you require?
<--- Score

72. What are the record-keeping requirements of investment priorities activities?
<--- Score

73. What is the scope of the investment priorities work?
<--- Score

74. Has a high-level 'as is' process map been completed, verified and validated?
<--- Score

75. Has a investment priorities requirement not been met?
<--- Score

76. Are all requirements met?
<--- Score

77. How is the team tracking and documenting its work?
<--- Score

78. Are there different segments of customers?
<--- Score

79. Is it clearly defined in and to your organization what you do?
<--- Score

80. Are roles and responsibilities formally defined?
<--- Score

81. How do you manage unclear investment priorities requirements?
<--- Score

82. Are audit criteria, scope, frequency and methods defined?
<--- Score

83. If substitutes have been appointed, have they been briefed on the investment priorities goals and received regular communications as to the progress to date?
<--- Score

84. What is the context?
<--- Score

85. What scope to assess?
<--- Score

86. What is the scope?
<--- Score

87. What is in the scope and what is not in scope?
<--- Score

88. What defines best in class?
<--- Score

89. How does the investment priorities manager ensure against scope creep?
<--- Score

90. Does the scope remain the same?
<--- Score

91. Is the investment priorities scope complete and appropriately sized?
<--- Score

92. Who is gathering investment priorities information?
<--- Score

93. Are the investment priorities requirements testable?
<--- Score

94. Have specific policy objectives been defined?
<--- Score

95. What critical content must be communicated – who, what, when, where, and how?
<--- Score

96. Are accountability and ownership for investment priorities clearly defined?
<--- Score

97. Who defines (or who defined) the rules and roles?
<--- Score

98. Is investment priorities currently on schedule according to the plan?

<--- Score

99. How often are the team meetings?
<--- Score

100. What is the definition of success?
<--- Score

101. What is in scope?
<--- Score

102. Who are the investment priorities improvement team members, including Management Leads and Coaches?
<--- Score

103. Is there a clear investment priorities case definition?
<--- Score

104. The political context: who holds power?
<--- Score

105. What sources do you use to gather information for a investment priorities study?
<--- Score

106. Has everyone on the team, including the team leaders, been properly trained?
<--- Score

107. Has the direction changed at all during the course of investment priorities? If so, when did it change and why?
<--- Score

108. How have you defined all investment priorities requirements first?
<--- Score

109. How will variation in the actual durations of each activity be dealt with to ensure that the expected investment priorities results are met?
<--- Score

110. How do you manage changes in investment priorities requirements?
<--- Score

111. Do you have a investment priorities success story or case study ready to tell and share?
<--- Score

112. Are task requirements clearly defined?
<--- Score

113. Are resources adequate for the scope?
<--- Score

114. Is the current 'as is' process being followed? If not, what are the discrepancies?
<--- Score

115. Do the problem and goal statements meet the SMART criteria (specific, measurable, attainable, relevant, and time-bound)?
<--- Score

116. What was the context?
<--- Score

117. What are the investment priorities use cases?

<--- Score

118. What investment priorities requirements should be gathered?
<--- Score

119. What would be the goal or target for a investment priorities's improvement team?
<--- Score

120. How do you manage scope?
<--- Score

121. Is scope creep really all bad news?
<--- Score

122. What are the tasks and definitions?
<--- Score

123. What are the rough order estimates on cost savings/opportunities that investment priorities brings?
<--- Score

124. Why are you doing investment priorities and what is the scope?
<--- Score

125. What system do you use for gathering investment priorities information?
<--- Score

126. What is out-of-scope initially?
<--- Score

127. Do you all define investment priorities in the

same way?

<--- Score

128. How would you define the culture at your organization, how susceptible is it to investment priorities changes?

<--- Score

129. Has/have the customer(s) been identified?

<--- Score

130. Are approval levels defined for contracts and supplements to contracts?

<--- Score

Add up total points for this section:

_ _ _ _ _ = Total points for this section

Divided by: _ _ _ _ _ _ (number of statements answered) = _ _ _ _ _ _ Average score for this section

Transfer your score to the investment priorities Index at the beginning of the Self-Assessment.

CRITERION #3: MEASURE:

INTENT: Gather the correct data.
Measure the current performance and
evolution of the situation.

In my belief, the answer to this
question is clearly defined:

5 Strongly Agree

4 Agree

3 Neutral

2 Disagree

1 Strongly Disagree

1. What are the costs and benefits?
<--- Score

2. How do you quantify and qualify impacts?
<--- Score

3. Are the investment priorities benefits worth its
costs?
<--- Score

4. How much does it cost?
<--- Score

5. What is the governance model that will address investment priorities, funding mechanisms, portfolio effectiveness, service levels for shared services, and adherence/compliance actions?
<--- Score

6. How will costs be allocated?
<--- Score

7. How do your measurements capture actionable investment priorities information for use in exceeding your customers expectations and securing your customers engagement?
<--- Score

8. What harm might be caused?
<--- Score

9. How are you verifying it?
<--- Score

10. What do you measure and why?
<--- Score

11. Have you included everything in your investment priorities cost models?
<--- Score

12. Are actual costs in line with budgeted costs?
<--- Score

13. What measurements are possible, practicable and

meaningful?
<--- Score

14. How do you verify if investment priorities is built right?
<--- Score

15. What drives O&M cost?
<--- Score

16. Are the units of measure consistent?
<--- Score

17. What is the root cause(s) of the problem?
<--- Score

18. What are the uncertainties surrounding estimates of impact?
<--- Score

19. How will you measure your investment priorities effectiveness?
<--- Score

20. What are allowable costs?
<--- Score

21. How will measures be used to manage and adapt?
<--- Score

22. What is an unallowable cost?
<--- Score

23. Where can you go to verify the info?
<--- Score

24. Are there measurements based on task performance?
<--- Score

25. How are costs allocated?
<--- Score

26. What does your operating model cost?
<--- Score

27. Does a investment priorities quantification method exist?
<--- Score

28. Which customer relationship and intelligence categories are urgent investment priorities?
<--- Score

29. At what cost?
<--- Score

30. Which customer workforce empowerment categories are urgent investment priorities?
<--- Score

31. What are the costs of delaying investment priorities action?
<--- Score

32. Which measures and indicators matter?
<--- Score

33. How do you verify and validate the investment priorities data?
<--- Score

34. What are the investment priorities key cost drivers?
<--- Score

35. Which investment priorities impacts are significant?
<--- Score

36. What is the governance model that will addresses investment priorities, funding mechanisms, portfolio effectiveness, service levels for share services, and adherence/compliance actions?
<--- Score

37. Does management have the right priorities among projects?
<--- Score

38. How will cloud computing, big data and mobility influence business models and investment priorities?
<--- Score

39. Are you aware of what could cause a problem?
<--- Score

40. What does verifying compliance entail?
<--- Score

41. How do you aggregate measures across priorities?
<--- Score

42. How to cause the change?
<--- Score

43. Who pays the cost?
<--- Score

44. Do you have any cost investment priorities limitation requirements?
<--- Score

45. What are your customers expectations and measures?
<--- Score

46. How frequently do you verify your investment priorities strategy?
<--- Score

47. How do you verify investment priorities completeness and accuracy?
<--- Score

48. Among the investment priorities product and service cost to be estimated, which is considered hardest to estimate?
<--- Score

49. What could cause delays in the schedule?
<--- Score

50. What causes investor action?
<--- Score

51. What is the total fixed cost?
<--- Score

52. Do you aggressively reward and promote the people who have the biggest impact on creating excellent investment priorities services/products?

<--- Score

53. How do you focus on what is right -not who is right?
<--- Score

54. Is there an opportunity to verify requirements?
<--- Score

55. What are the estimated costs of proposed changes?
<--- Score

56. How is progress measured?
<--- Score

57. Do the benefits outweigh the costs?
<--- Score

58. What does a Test Case verify?
<--- Score

59. How can a investment priorities test verify your ideas or assumptions?
<--- Score

60. How can you manage cost down?
<--- Score

61. How do you verify and develop ideas and innovations?
<--- Score

62. How is the value delivered by investment priorities being measured?
<--- Score

63. Are investment priorities vulnerabilities categorized and prioritized?
<--- Score

64. Where is the cost?
<--- Score

65. What are the types and number of measures to use?
<--- Score

66. How do you verify performance?
<--- Score

67. How do you verify your resources?
<--- Score

68. Are missed investment priorities opportunities costing your organization money?
<--- Score

69. What is the investment priorities business impact?
<--- Score

70. What relevant entities could be measured?
<--- Score

71. What is measured? Why?
<--- Score

72. How do you measure variability?
<--- Score

73. Who should receive measurement reports?
<--- Score

74. What are hidden investment priorities quality costs?

<--- Score

75. What do people want to verify?

<--- Score

76. What are the current costs of the investment priorities process?

<--- Score

77. How can you reduce costs?

<--- Score

78. What details are required of the investment priorities cost structure?

<--- Score

79. How will cloud computing, big data and mobility influence I&O business models and investment priorities?

<--- Score

80. What are the strategic priorities for this year?

<--- Score

81. How do you prevent mis-estimating cost?

<--- Score

82. What would it cost to replace your technology?

<--- Score

83. Is the solution cost-effective?

<--- Score

84. What can be used to verify compliance?
<--- Score

85. What are your primary costs, revenues, assets?
<--- Score

86. What is the cause of any investment priorities gaps?
<--- Score

87. Are supply costs steady or fluctuating?
<--- Score

88. What is the cost of rework?
<--- Score

89. The approach of traditional investment priorities works for detail complexity but is focused on a systematic approach rather than an understanding of the nature of systems themselves, what approach will permit your organization to deal with the kind of unpredictable emergent behaviors that dynamic complexity can introduce?
<--- Score

90. What are your key investment priorities organizational performance measures, including key short and longer-term financial measures?
<--- Score

91. What are the operational costs after investment priorities deployment?
<--- Score

92. Are you able to realize any cost savings?
<--- Score

93. Do you verify that corrective actions were taken?
<--- Score

94. Have design-to-cost goals been established?
<--- Score

95. What is the total cost related to deploying investment priorities, including any consulting or professional services?
<--- Score

96. Why do the measurements/indicators matter?
<--- Score

97. How do you measure lifecycle phases?
<--- Score

98. Is the cost worth the investment priorities effort ?
<--- Score

99. What causes extra work or rework?
<--- Score

100. Will investment priorities have an impact on current business continuity, disaster recovery processes and/or infrastructure?
<--- Score

101. Why a investment priorities focus?
<--- Score

102. Have you made assumptions about the shape of the future, particularly its impact on your customers and competitors?
<--- Score

103. How do you control the overall costs of your work processes?
<--- Score

104. What are the investment priorities investment costs?
<--- Score

105. Did you tackle the cause or the symptom?
<--- Score

106. How do you measure efficient delivery of investment priorities services?
<--- Score

107. Are the measurements objective?
<--- Score

108. How sensitive must the investment priorities strategy be to cost?
<--- Score

109. What potential environmental factors impact the investment priorities effort?
<--- Score

110. How are measurements made?
<--- Score

111. How can you reduce the costs of obtaining inputs?
<--- Score

112. What is your investment priorities quality cost segregation study?

<--- Score

113. How do you verify the investment priorities requirements quality?
<--- Score

114. How do you stay flexible and focused to recognize larger investment priorities results?
<--- Score

115. Has a cost center been established?
<--- Score

116. How will effects be measured?
<--- Score

117. How frequently do you track investment priorities measures?
<--- Score

118. Are you taking your company in the direction of better and revenue or cheaper and cost?
<--- Score

119. What users will be impacted?
<--- Score

120. Was a business case (cost/benefit) developed?
<--- Score

121. How do you verify the authenticity of the data and information used?
<--- Score

122. Is it possible to estimate the impact of unanticipated complexity such as wrong or failed

assumptions, feedback, etcetera on proposed reforms?
<--- Score

123. How long to keep data and how to manage retention costs?
<--- Score

124. How can you measure investment priorities in a systematic way?
<--- Score

125. Where is it measured?
<--- Score

126. What are your operating costs?
<--- Score

127. How will your organization measure success?
<--- Score

128. What methods are feasible and acceptable to estimate the impact of reforms?
<--- Score

129. What causes mismanagement?
<--- Score

130. What evidence is there and what is measured?
<--- Score

131. What are you verifying?
<--- Score

132. Do you have an issue in getting priority?
<--- Score

133. When a disaster occurs, who gets priority?
<--- Score

134. What would be a real cause for concern?
<--- Score

135. What disadvantage does this cause for the user?
<--- Score

136. How will success or failure be measured?
<--- Score

137. Why do you expend time and effort to implement measurement, for whom?
<--- Score

138. How can you measure the performance?
<--- Score

139. What are the costs?
<--- Score

140. Which costs should be taken into account?
<--- Score

141. How will you measure success?
<--- Score

Add up total points for this section:
_ _ _ _ _ = Total points for this section

Divided by: _ _ _ _ _ _ (number of
statements answered) = _ _ _ _ _ _
Average score for this section

Transfer your score to the investment priorities Index at the beginning of the Self-Assessment.

CRITERION #4: ANALYZE:

INTENT: Analyze causes, assumptions and hypotheses.

In my belief, the answer to this question is clearly defined:

5 Strongly Agree

4 Agree

3 Neutral

2 Disagree

1 Strongly Disagree

1. What data is gathered?
<--- Score

2. What, related to, investment priorities processes does your organization outsource?
<--- Score

3. Where can you get qualified talent today?
<--- Score

4. What other jobs or tasks affect the performance of the steps in the investment priorities process?
<--- Score

5. What were the crucial 'moments of truth' on the process map?
<--- Score

6. How do you use investment priorities data and information to support organizational decision making and innovation?
<--- Score

7. What other organizational variables, such as reward systems or communication systems, affect the performance of this investment priorities process?
<--- Score

8. What are the revised rough estimates of the financial savings/opportunity for investment priorities improvements?
<--- Score

9. Were there any improvement opportunities identified from the process analysis?
<--- Score

10. What resources go in to get the desired output?
<--- Score

11. Is the final output clearly identified?
<--- Score

12. What types of data do your investment priorities indicators require?
<--- Score

13. How do you ensure that the investment priorities opportunity is realistic?
<--- Score

14. How has the investment priorities data been gathered?
<--- Score

15. What are your investment priorities processes?
<--- Score

16. How difficult is it to qualify what investment priorities ROI is?
<--- Score

17. What are the best opportunities for value improvement?
<--- Score

18. What is the cost of poor quality as supported by the team's analysis?
<--- Score

19. Are investment priorities changes recognized early enough to be approved through the regular process?
<--- Score

20. Do your employees have the opportunity to do what they do best everyday?
<--- Score

21. How do mission and objectives affect the investment priorities processes of your organization?
<--- Score

22. Who owns what data?

<--- Score

23. Is the performance gap determined?

<--- Score

24. What are the investment priorities design outputs?

<--- Score

25. What are evaluation criteria for the output?

<--- Score

26. What process improvements will be needed?

<--- Score

27. What qualifications do investment priorities leaders need?

<--- Score

28. Which investment priorities data should be retained?

<--- Score

29. Were Pareto charts (or similar) used to portray the 'heavy hitters' (or key sources of variation)?

<--- Score

30. Where is the data coming from to measure compliance?

<--- Score

31. Do staff qualifications match your project?

<--- Score

32. What output to create?

<--- Score

33. How will corresponding data be collected?
<--- Score

34. What are the necessary qualifications?
<--- Score

35. What investment priorities data should be managed?
<--- Score

36. Who will gather what data?
<--- Score

37. What information qualified as important?
<--- Score

38. Are all staff in core investment priorities subjects Highly Qualified?
<--- Score

39. How can risk management be tied procedurally to process elements?
<--- Score

40. What conclusions were drawn from the team's data collection and analysis? How did the team reach these conclusions?
<--- Score

41. An organizationally feasible system request is one that considers the mission, goals and objectives of the organization, key questions are: is the investment priorities solution request practical and will it solve a problem or take advantage of an opportunity to achieve company goals?

<--- Score

42. How do your work systems and key work processes relate to and capitalize on your core competencies?
<--- Score

43. What is your organizations process which leads to recognition of value generation?
<--- Score

44. What is the Value Stream Mapping?
<--- Score

45. Is there any way to speed up the process?
<--- Score

46. How do you identify specific investment priorities investment opportunities and emerging trends?
<--- Score

47. What did the team gain from developing a sub-process map?
<--- Score

48. Was a cause-and-effect diagram used to explore the different types of causes (or sources of variation)?
<--- Score

49. Were any designed experiments used to generate additional insight into the data analysis?
<--- Score

50. What tools were used to narrow the list of possible causes?
<--- Score

51. What investment priorities data do you gather or use now?
<--- Score

52. What internal processes need improvement?
<--- Score

53. What is the complexity of the output produced?
<--- Score

54. How was the detailed process map generated, verified, and validated?
<--- Score

55. Think about some of the processes you undertake within your organization, which do you own?
<--- Score

56. Is there a strict change management process?
<--- Score

57. Who is involved with workflow mapping?
<--- Score

58. How is the data gathered?
<--- Score

59. What are your current levels and trends in key investment priorities measures or indicators of product and process performance that are important to and directly serve your customers?
<--- Score

60. What investment priorities data should be collected?

<--- Score

61. When should a process be art not science?
<--- Score

62. How is data used for program management and improvement?
<--- Score

63. What kind of crime could a potential new hire have committed that would not only not disqualify him/her from being hired by your organization, but would actually indicate that he/she might be a particularly good fit?
<--- Score

64. Have the problem and goal statements been updated to reflect the additional knowledge gained from the analyze phase?
<--- Score

65. How will the investment priorities data be captured?
<--- Score

66. How are outputs preserved and protected?
<--- Score

67. What systems/processes must you excel at?
<--- Score

68. Are your outputs consistent?
<--- Score

69. Where is investment priorities data gathered?
<--- Score

70. What is your organizations system for selecting qualified vendors?
<--- Score

71. What is the output?
<--- Score

72. Is the required investment priorities data gathered?
<--- Score

73. What qualifications are needed?
<--- Score

74. Should you invest in industry-recognized qualifications?
<--- Score

75. What are the processes for audit reporting and management?
<--- Score

76. What qualifies as competition?
<--- Score

77. Who will facilitate the team and process?
<--- Score

78. Think about the functions involved in your investment priorities project, what processes flow from these functions?
<--- Score

79. What qualifications and skills do you need?
<--- Score

80. What controls do you have in place to protect data?
<--- Score

81. Do quality systems drive continuous improvement?
<--- Score

82. Do several people in different organizational units assist with the investment priorities process?
<--- Score

83. Is the investment priorities process severely broken such that a re-design is necessary?
<--- Score

84. How is the way you as the leader think and process information affecting your organizational culture?
<--- Score

85. What is the investment priorities Driver?
<--- Score

86. Who is involved in the management review process?
<--- Score

87. Who qualifies to gain access to data?
<--- Score

88. Did any value-added analysis or 'lean thinking' take place to identify some of the gaps shown on the 'as is' process map?
<--- Score

89. Was a detailed process map created to amplify critical steps of the 'as is' stakeholder process?
<--- Score

90. Is data and process analysis, root cause analysis and quantifying the gap/opportunity in place?
<--- Score

91. How much data can be collected in the given timeframe?
<--- Score

92. How many input/output points does it require?
<--- Score

93. Do your leaders quickly bounce back from setbacks?
<--- Score

94. What are the investment priorities business drivers?
<--- Score

95. What are the personnel training and qualifications required?
<--- Score

96. What investment priorities metrics are outputs of the process?
<--- Score

97. How do you promote understanding that opportunity for improvement is not criticism of the status quo, or the people who created the status quo?
<--- Score

98. What are your current levels and trends in key measures or indicators of investment priorities product and process performance that are important to and directly serve your customers? How do these results compare with the performance of your competitors and other organizations with similar offerings?
<--- Score

99. How does the organization define, manage, and improve its investment priorities processes?
<--- Score

100. Is pre-qualification of suppliers carried out?
<--- Score

101. A compounding model resolution with available relevant data can often provide insight towards a solution methodology; which investment priorities models, tools and techniques are necessary?
<--- Score

102. What investment priorities data will be collected?
<--- Score

103. How is the investment priorities Value Stream Mapping managed?
<--- Score

104. What are your best practices for minimizing investment priorities project risk, while demonstrating incremental value and quick wins throughout the investment priorities project lifecycle?
<--- Score

105. What training and qualifications will you need?

<--- Score

106. How do you implement and manage your work processes to ensure that they meet design requirements?
<--- Score

107. What successful thing are you doing today that may be blinding you to new growth opportunities?
<--- Score

108. What were the financial benefits resulting from any 'ground fruit or low-hanging fruit' (quick fixes)?
<--- Score

109. Has data output been validated?
<--- Score

110. What methods do you use to gather investment priorities data?
<--- Score

111. How do you define collaboration and team output?
<--- Score

112. Are gaps between current performance and the goal performance identified?
<--- Score

113. What tools were used to generate the list of possible causes?
<--- Score

114. Do you understand your management processes today?

<--- Score

115. What are your key performance measures or indicators and in-process measures for the control and improvement of your investment priorities processes?
<--- Score

116. What process should you select for improvement?
<--- Score

117. Have you defined which data is gathered how?
<--- Score

118. Has an output goal been set?
<--- Score

119. How will the data be checked for quality?
<--- Score

120. Can you add value to the current investment priorities decision-making process (largely qualitative) by incorporating uncertainty modeling (more quantitative)?
<--- Score

121. Do your contracts/agreements contain data security obligations?
<--- Score

122. What do you need to qualify?
<--- Score

123. Do you have the authority to produce the output?

<--- Score

124. What does the data say about the performance of the stakeholder process?
<--- Score

125. Did any additional data need to be collected?
<--- Score

126. How is investment priorities data gathered?
<--- Score

127. What are the disruptive investment priorities technologies that enable your organization to radically change your business processes?
<--- Score

128. Is the gap/opportunity displayed and communicated in financial terms?
<--- Score

129. What quality tools were used to get through the analyze phase?
<--- Score

130. Are all team members qualified for all tasks?
<--- Score

131. What is the oversight process?
<--- Score

132. Have any additional benefits been identified that will result from closing all or most of the gaps?
<--- Score

133. Do you, as a leader, bounce back quickly from

setbacks?

<--- Score

134. What are your outputs?

<--- Score

135. Are you missing investment priorities opportunities?

<--- Score

Add up total points for this section:
_ _ _ _ _ = Total points for this section

Divided by: _ _ _ _ _ _ (number of statements answered) = _ _ _ _ _ _
Average score for this section

Transfer your score to the investment priorities Index at the beginning of the Self-Assessment.

CRITERION #5: IMPROVE:

INTENT: Develop a practical solution. Innovate, establish and test the solution and to measure the results.

In my belief, the answer to this question is clearly defined:

5 Strongly Agree

4 Agree

3 Neutral

2 Disagree

1 Strongly Disagree

1. How does your organization evaluate strategic investment priorities success?
<--- Score

2. What tools were used to evaluate the potential solutions?
<--- Score

3. What tools were used to tap into the creativity and

encourage 'outside the box' thinking?
<--- Score

4. Are the most efficient solutions problem-specific?
<--- Score

5. What actually has to improve and by how much?
<--- Score

6. What is investment priorities's impact on utilizing the best solution(s)?
<--- Score

7. Why improve in the first place?
<--- Score

8. Is the investment priorities documentation thorough?
<--- Score

9. Do those selected for the investment priorities team have a good general understanding of what investment priorities is all about?
<--- Score

10. Where do you need investment priorities improvement?
<--- Score

11. For decision problems, how do you develop a decision statement?
<--- Score

12. How scalable is your investment priorities solution?
<--- Score

13. Who manages supplier risk management in your organization?
<--- Score

14. How can you improve investment priorities?
<--- Score

15. How do you manage and improve your investment priorities work systems to deliver customer value and achieve organizational success and sustainability?
<--- Score

16. Who are the people involved in developing and implementing investment priorities?
<--- Score

17. What alternative responses are available to manage risk?
<--- Score

18. Do vendor agreements bring new compliance risk ?
<--- Score

19. Who will be using the results of the measurement activities?
<--- Score

20. Which investment priorities solution is appropriate?
<--- Score

21. Are the key business and technology risks being managed?

<--- Score

22. How do you measure improved investment priorities service perception, and satisfaction?
<--- Score

23. What practices helps your organization to develop its capacity to recognize patterns?
<--- Score

24. What lessons, if any, from a pilot were incorporated into the design of the full-scale solution?
<--- Score

25. What are the concrete investment priorities results?
<--- Score

26. Can you integrate quality management and risk management?
<--- Score

27. Who makes the investment priorities decisions in your organization?
<--- Score

28. Is supporting investment priorities documentation required?
<--- Score

29. What is investment priorities risk?
<--- Score

30. What are the implications of the one critical investment priorities decision 10 minutes, 10 months, and 10 years from now?

<--- Score

31. Who do you report investment priorities results
to?
<--- Score

32. Are risk management tasks balanced centrally and
locally?
<--- Score

33. Have you achieved investment priorities
improvements?
<--- Score

34. What are your current levels and trends in key
measures or indicators of workforce and leader
development?
<--- Score

35. Is risk periodically assessed?
<--- Score

36. To what extent does management recognize
investment priorities as a tool to increase the results?
<--- Score

37. What resources are required for the improvement
efforts?
<--- Score

38. What do you want to improve?
<--- Score

39. Do you combine technical expertise with
business knowledge and investment priorities Key
topics include lifecycles, development approaches,

requirements and how to make a business case?
<--- Score

40. investment priorities risk decisions: whose call Is
It?
<--- Score

41. What criteria will you use to assess your
investment priorities risks?
<--- Score

42. What tools do you use once you have decided on
a investment priorities strategy and more importantly
how do you choose?
<--- Score

43. Who should make the investment priorities
decisions?
<--- Score

44. Can you identify any significant risks or exposures
to investment priorities third- parties (vendors, service
providers, alliance partners etc) that concern you?
<--- Score

45. At what point will vulnerability assessments be
performed once investment priorities is put into
production (e.g., ongoing Risk Management after
implementation)?
<--- Score

46. How is continuous improvement applied to risk
management?
<--- Score

47. What investment priorities improvements can be

made?
<--- Score

48. How will you recognize and celebrate results?
<--- Score

49. What should a proof of concept or pilot accomplish?
<--- Score

50. How is knowledge sharing about risk management improved?
<--- Score

51. What does the 'should be' process map/design look like?
<--- Score

52. What is the magnitude of the improvements?
<--- Score

53. If you could go back in time five years, what decision would you make differently? What is your best guess as to what decision you're making today you might regret five years from now?
<--- Score

54. Are the risks fully understood, reasonable and manageable?
<--- Score

55. How do you measure progress and evaluate training effectiveness?
<--- Score

56. What is the risk?

<--- Score

57. What is the implementation plan?
<--- Score

58. What went well, what should change, what can improve?
<--- Score

59. Are risk triggers captured?
<--- Score

60. How do you improve investment priorities service perception, and satisfaction?
<--- Score

61. How will you know that a change is an improvement?
<--- Score

62. How are investment priorities risks managed?
<--- Score

63. Is investment priorities documentation maintained?
<--- Score

64. What risks do you need to manage?
<--- Score

65. Is any investment priorities documentation required?
<--- Score

66. Is the measure of success for investment priorities understandable to a variety of people?

<--- Score

67. Risk Identification: What are the possible risk events your organization faces in relation to investment priorities?
<--- Score

68. What can you do to improve?
<--- Score

69. Risk factors: what are the characteristics of investment priorities that make it risky?
<--- Score

70. Who manages investment priorities risk?
<--- Score

71. How risky is your organization?
<--- Score

72. Who will be responsible for making the decisions to include or exclude requested changes once investment priorities is underway?
<--- Score

73. What is the investment priorities's sustainability risk?
<--- Score

74. How can you improve performance?
<--- Score

75. What current systems have to be understood and/ or changed?
<--- Score

76. Is the scope clearly documented?
<--- Score

77. Who are the investment priorities decision makers?
<--- Score

78. Will the controls trigger any other risks?
<--- Score

79. Is there a high likelihood that any recommendations will achieve their intended results?
<--- Score

80. How do you keep improving investment priorities?
<--- Score

81. What error proofing will be done to address some of the discrepancies observed in the 'as is' process?
<--- Score

82. Who are the investment priorities decision-makers?
<--- Score

83. How do you link measurement and risk?
<--- Score

84. Is the investment priorities solution sustainable?
<--- Score

85. Who will be responsible for documenting the investment priorities requirements in detail?
<--- Score

86. Is there any other investment priorities solution?

<--- Score

87. Are events managed to resolution?
<--- Score

88. How are policy decisions made and where?
<--- Score

89. What is the team's contingency plan for potential problems occurring in implementation?
<--- Score

90. Is the solution technically practical?
<--- Score

91. How do you measure risk?
<--- Score

92. Are you assessing investment priorities and risk?
<--- Score

93. What strategies for investment priorities improvement are successful?
<--- Score

94. How do you define the solutions' scope?
<--- Score

95. How do you mitigate investment priorities risk?
<--- Score

96. What area needs the greatest improvement?
<--- Score

97. How do you manage investment priorities risk?
<--- Score

98. How do you improve your likelihood of success ?
<--- Score

99. Which of the recognised risks out of all risks can be most likely transferred?
<--- Score

100. Who are the key stakeholders for the investment priorities evaluation?
<--- Score

101. What assumptions are made about the solution and approach?
<--- Score

102. How will you know when its improved?
<--- Score

103. How do you decide how much to remunerate an employee?
<--- Score

104. Are procedures documented for managing investment priorities risks?
<--- Score

105. How do you deal with investment priorities risk?
<--- Score

106. Do you cover the five essential competencies: Communication, Collaboration,Innovation, Adaptability, and Leadership that improve an organizations ability to leverage the new investment priorities in a volatile global economy?
<--- Score

107. Can the solution be designed and implemented within an acceptable time period?
<--- Score

108. How does the team improve its work?
<--- Score

109. Would you develop a investment priorities Communication Strategy?
<--- Score

110. How do you improve productivity?
<--- Score

111. Are decisions made in a timely manner?
<--- Score

112. Risk events: what are the things that could go wrong?
<--- Score

113. Do you have the optimal project management team structure?
<--- Score

114. What tools were most useful during the improve phase?
<--- Score

115. How significant is the improvement in the eyes of the end user?
<--- Score

116. When you map the key players in your own work and the types/domains of relationships with them,

which relationships do you find easy and which
challenging, and why?
<--- Score

117. Do you need to do a usability evaluation?
<--- Score

118. Explorations of the frontiers of investment
priorities will help you build influence, improve
investment priorities, optimize decision making, and
sustain change, what is your approach?
<--- Score

119. What are the affordable investment priorities
risks?
<--- Score

120. How can skill-level changes improve investment
priorities?
<--- Score

121. For estimation problems, how do you develop an
estimation statement?
<--- Score

122. Was a investment priorities charter developed?
<--- Score

123. What improvements have been achieved?
<--- Score

124. Have you identified breakpoints and/or risk
tolerances that will trigger broad consideration of
a potential need for intervention or modification of
strategy?
<--- Score

125. Who controls key decisions that will be made?
<--- Score

126. Where do the investment priorities decisions reside?
<--- Score

127. Does a good decision guarantee a good outcome?
<--- Score

128. Who controls the risk?
<--- Score

129. What were the underlying assumptions on the cost-benefit analysis?
<--- Score

130. What are the investment priorities security risks?
<--- Score

131. What are the expected investment priorities results?
<--- Score

132. How do you go about comparing investment priorities approaches/solutions?
<--- Score

133. Is the investment priorities risk managed?
<--- Score

134. What needs improvement? Why?
<--- Score

Add up total points for this section:
_____ = Total points for this section

Divided by: _____ (number of
statements answered) = _____
Average score for this section

Transfer your score to the investment
priorities Index at the beginning of the
Self-Assessment.

CRITERION #6: CONTROL:

INTENT: Implement the practical
solution. Maintain the performance and
correct possible complications.

In my belief, the answer to this
question is clearly defined:

5 Strongly Agree

4 Agree

3 Neutral

2 Disagree

1 Strongly Disagree

1. What is your theory of human motivation, and how does your compensation plan fit with that view?
<--- Score

2. Can you adapt and adjust to changing investment priorities situations?
<--- Score

3. Does the investment priorities performance meet

the customer's requirements?
<--- Score

4. In the case of a investment priorities project, the criteria for the audit derive from implementation objectives, an audit of a investment priorities project involves assessing whether the recommendations outlined for implementation have been met, can you track that any investment priorities project is implemented as planned, and is it working?
<--- Score

5. Are pertinent alerts monitored, analyzed and distributed to appropriate personnel?
<--- Score

6. Are operating procedures consistent?
<--- Score

7. How might the group capture best practices and lessons learned so as to leverage improvements?
<--- Score

8. Will the team be available to assist members in planning investigations?
<--- Score

9. How will report readings be checked to effectively monitor performance?
<--- Score

10. Is a response plan in place for when the input, process, or output measures indicate an 'out-of-control' condition?
<--- Score

11. What are the known security controls?
<--- Score

12. Act/Adjust: What Do you Need to Do Differently?
<--- Score

13. How will input, process, and output variables be
checked to detect for sub-optimal conditions?
<--- Score

14. Does investment priorities appropriately measure
and monitor risk?
<--- Score

15. Do you monitor the effectiveness of your
investment priorities activities?
<--- Score

16. What other systems, operations, processes, and
infrastructures (hiring practices, staffing, training,
incentives/rewards, metrics/dashboards/scorecards,
etc.) need updates, additions, changes, or deletions
in order to facilitate knowledge transfer and
improvements?
<--- Score

17. What do your reports reflect?
<--- Score

18. Who sets the investment priorities standards?
<--- Score

19. How do senior leaders actions reflect a
commitment to the organizations investment
priorities values?
<--- Score

20. Is there documentation that will support the successful operation of the improvement?
<--- Score

21. How can you best use all of your knowledge repositories to enhance learning and sharing?
<--- Score

22. What other areas of the group might benefit from the investment priorities team's improvements, knowledge, and learning?
<--- Score

23. What should you measure to verify efficiency gains?
<--- Score

24. Is there an action plan in case of emergencies?
<--- Score

25. Implementation Planning: is a pilot needed to test the changes before a full roll out occurs?
<--- Score

26. How do you spread information?
<--- Score

27. How will the process owner and team be able to hold the gains?
<--- Score

28. Is reporting being used or needed?
<--- Score

29. Has the improved process and its steps been

standardized?
<--- Score

30. How is change control managed?
<--- Score

31. Are suggested corrective/restorative actions indicated on the response plan for known causes to problems that might surface?
<--- Score

32. Is knowledge gained on process shared and institutionalized?
<--- Score

33. What is the standard for acceptable investment priorities performance?
<--- Score

34. Will any special training be provided for results interpretation?
<--- Score

35. Where do ideas that reach policy makers and planners as proposals for investment priorities strengthening and reform actually originate?
<--- Score

36. Against what alternative is success being measured?
<--- Score

37. Is the investment priorities test/monitoring cost justified?
<--- Score

38. Is there a control plan in place for sustaining improvements (short and long-term)?
<--- Score

39. Will existing staff require re-training, for example, to learn new business processes?
<--- Score

40. Who is the investment priorities process owner?
<--- Score

41. How do you encourage people to take control and responsibility?
<--- Score

42. How will the day-to-day responsibilities for monitoring and continual improvement be transferred from the improvement team to the process owner?
<--- Score

43. What are you attempting to measure/monitor?
<--- Score

44. How do controls support value?
<--- Score

45. Are there documented procedures?
<--- Score

46. What do you stand for--and what are you against?
<--- Score

47. Do you monitor the investment priorities decisions made and fine tune them as they evolve?
<--- Score

48. How will investment priorities decisions be made and monitored?
<--- Score

49. Have new or revised work instructions resulted?
<--- Score

50. What adjustments to the strategies are needed?
<--- Score

51. Are the investment priorities standards challenging?
<--- Score

52. Who will be in control?
<--- Score

53. How do you plan for the cost of succession?
<--- Score

54. How do your controls stack up?
<--- Score

55. What can you control?
<--- Score

56. What should the next improvement project be that is related to investment priorities?
<--- Score

57. Is there a transfer of ownership and knowledge to process owner and process team tasked with the responsibilities.
<--- Score

58. What are your results for key measures or indicators of the accomplishment of your investment priorities strategy and action plans, including building and strengthening core competencies?
<--- Score

59. You may have created your quality measures at a time when you lacked resources, technology wasn't up to the required standard, or low service levels were the industry norm. Have those circumstances changed?
<--- Score

60. What is the best design framework for investment priorities organization now that, in a post industrial-age if the top-down, command and control model is no longer relevant?
<--- Score

61. Do the investment priorities decisions you make today help people and the planet tomorrow?
<--- Score

62. Does a troubleshooting guide exist or is it needed?
<--- Score

63. Is a response plan established and deployed?
<--- Score

64. Is new knowledge gained imbedded in the response plan?
<--- Score

65. What is your plan to assess your security risks?
<--- Score

66. What are the critical parameters to watch?
<--- Score

67. Who is going to spread your message?
<--- Score

68. Is there a recommended audit plan for routine surveillance inspections of investment priorities's gains?
<--- Score

69. What is the recommended frequency of auditing?
<--- Score

70. Will your goals reflect your program budget?
<--- Score

71. What is the control/monitoring plan?
<--- Score

72. Does job training on the documented procedures need to be part of the process team's education and training?
<--- Score

73. What are the performance and scale of the investment priorities tools?
<--- Score

74. Are controls in place and consistently applied?
<--- Score

75. How likely is the current investment priorities plan to come in on schedule or on budget?
<--- Score

76. Can support from partners be adjusted?
<--- Score

77. Has the investment priorities value of standards been quantified?
<--- Score

78. What key inputs and outputs are being measured on an ongoing basis?
<--- Score

79. How will the process owner verify improvement in present and future sigma levels, process capabilities?
<--- Score

80. Does the response plan contain a definite closed loop continual improvement scheme (e.g., plan-do-check-act)?
<--- Score

81. Is there a standardized process?
<--- Score

82. How is investment priorities project cost planned, managed, monitored?
<--- Score

83. Is there a documented and implemented monitoring plan?
<--- Score

84. How do you monitor usage and cost?
<--- Score

85. How will new or emerging customer needs/requirements be checked/communicated to orient

the process toward meeting the new specifications and continually reducing variation?
<--- Score

86. What are the key elements of your investment priorities performance improvement system, including your evaluation, organizational learning, and innovation processes?
<--- Score

87. How widespread is its use?
<--- Score

88. Are the planned controls working?
<--- Score

89. Do the viable solutions scale to future needs?
<--- Score

90. Are new process steps, standards, and documentation ingrained into normal operations?
<--- Score

91. What quality tools were useful in the control phase?
<--- Score

92. Is there a investment priorities Communication plan covering who needs to get what information when?
<--- Score

93. How do you select, collect, align, and integrate investment priorities data and information for tracking daily operations and overall organizational performance, including progress relative to strategic

objectives and action plans?
<--- Score

94. Are documented procedures clear and easy to
follow for the operators?
<--- Score

95. How do you establish and deploy modified action
plans if circumstances require a shift in plans and
rapid execution of new plans?
<--- Score

Add up total points for this section:
_____ = Total points for this section

Divided by: _____ (number of
statements answered) = _____
Average score for this section

Transfer your score to the investment
priorities Index at the beginning of the
Self-Assessment.

CRITERION #7: SUSTAIN:

1. What are you challenging?
<--- Score

2. How are you doing compared to your industry?
<--- Score

3. Who do you think the world wants your
organization to be?
<--- Score

4. How do you cross-sell and up-sell your investment

priorities success?
<--- Score

5. What is your competitive advantage?
<--- Score

6. How do you foster the skills, knowledge, talents, attributes, and characteristics you want to have?
<--- Score

7. What are the business goals investment priorities is aiming to achieve?
<--- Score

8. Why not do investment priorities?
<--- Score

9. What projects are going on in the organization today, and what resources are those projects using from the resource pools?
<--- Score

10. How can you become more high-tech but still be high touch?
<--- Score

11. How will you ensure you get what you expected?
<--- Score

12. What should you stop doing?
<--- Score

13. What are current investment priorities paradigms?
<--- Score

14. How do you accomplish your long range

investment priorities goals?
<--- Score

15. What relationships among investment priorities trends do you perceive?
<--- Score

16. Is there a work around that you can use?
<--- Score

17. How will you know that the investment priorities project has been successful?
<--- Score

18. Are you making progress, and are you making progress as investment priorities leaders?
<--- Score

19. Who else should you help?
<--- Score

20. What is your question? Why?
<--- Score

21. Which functions and people interact with the supplier and or customer?
<--- Score

22. Would you rather sell to knowledgeable and informed customers or to uninformed customers?
<--- Score

23. How do you keep records, of what?
<--- Score

24. What is your investment priorities strategy?

<--- Score

25. Is investment priorities dependent on the successful delivery of a current project?
<--- Score

26. Can you do all this work?
<--- Score

27. To whom do you add value?
<--- Score

28. What new services of functionality will be implemented next with investment priorities ?
<--- Score

29. What unique value proposition (UVP) do you offer?
<--- Score

30. Who are the key stakeholders?
<--- Score

31. If there were zero limitations, what would you do differently?
<--- Score

32. How do you proactively clarify deliverables and investment priorities quality expectations?
<--- Score

33. If you had to leave your organization for a year and the only communication you could have with employees/colleagues was a single paragraph, what would you write?
<--- Score

34. Is investment priorities realistic, or are you setting yourself up for failure?
<--- Score

35. If you got fired and a new hire took your place, what would she do different?
<--- Score

36. What are the long-term investment priorities goals?
<--- Score

37. What investment priorities skills are most important?
<--- Score

38. What goals did you miss?
<--- Score

39. What happens if you do not have enough funding?
<--- Score

40. Do you have the right capabilities and capacities?
<--- Score

41. What information is critical to your organization that your executives are ignoring?
<--- Score

42. How do you assess the investment priorities pitfalls that are inherent in implementing it?
<--- Score

43. How do you engage the workforce, in addition to satisfying them?

<--- Score

44. What may be the consequences for the performance of an organization if all stakeholders are not consulted regarding investment priorities?
<--- Score

45. What must you excel at?
<--- Score

46. Who do you want your customers to become?
<--- Score

47. What would you recommend your friend do if he/she were facing this dilemma?
<--- Score

48. Do you think investment priorities accomplishes the goals you expect it to accomplish?
<--- Score

49. Which investment priorities goals are the most important?
<--- Score

50. In the past year, what have you done (or could you have done) to increase the accurate perception of your company/brand as ethical and honest?
<--- Score

51. Do you say no to customers for no reason?
<--- Score

52. Whose voice (department, ethnic group, women, older workers, etc) might you have missed hearing from in your company, and how might you amplify

this voice to create positive momentum for your business?
<--- Score

53. Why will customers want to buy your organizations products/services?
<--- Score

54. How do you go about securing investment priorities?
<--- Score

55. What are the short and long-term investment priorities goals?
<--- Score

56. Who do we want your customers to become?
<--- Score

57. What trouble can you get into?
<--- Score

58. How do you stay inspired?
<--- Score

59. How do you transition from the baseline to the target?
<--- Score

60. When information truly is ubiquitous, when reach and connectivity are completely global, when computing resources are infinite, and when a whole new set of impossibilities are not only possible, but happening, what will that do to your business?
<--- Score

61. What are the barriers to increased investment priorities production?
<--- Score

62. What is the overall business strategy?
<--- Score

63. What is effective investment priorities?
<--- Score

64. Is there any reason to believe the opposite of my current belief?
<--- Score

65. If your customer were your grandmother, would you tell her to buy what you're selling?
<--- Score

66. Why do and why don't your customers like your organization?
<--- Score

67. How do you maintain investment priorities's Integrity?
<--- Score

68. How do you set investment priorities stretch targets and how do you get people to not only participate in setting these stretch targets but also that they strive to achieve these?
<--- Score

69. What one word do you want to own in the minds of your customers, employees, and partners?
<--- Score

70. What have been your experiences in defining long range investment priorities goals?
<--- Score

71. Is your basic point _____ or _____?
<--- Score

72. If you had to rebuild your organization without any traditional competitive advantages (i.e., no killer technology, promising research, innovative product/service delivery model, etcetera), how would your people have to approach their work and collaborate together in order to create the necessary conditions for success?
<--- Score

73. Marketing budgets are tighter, consumers are more skeptical, and social media has changed forever the way we talk about investment priorities, how do you gain traction?
<--- Score

74. What is a feasible sequencing of reform initiatives over time?
<--- Score

75. How do customers see your organization?
<--- Score

76. How can you negotiate investment priorities successfully with a stubborn boss, an irate client, or a deceitful coworker?
<--- Score

77. What investment priorities modifications can you make work for you?

<--- Score

78. What is it like to work for you?
<--- Score

79. How do you foster innovation?
<--- Score

80. Are you maintaining a past–present–future perspective throughout the investment priorities discussion?
<--- Score

81. What you are going to do to affect the numbers?
<--- Score

82. What are specific investment priorities rules to follow?
<--- Score

83. How is implementation research currently incorporated into each of your goals?
<--- Score

84. What will be the consequences to the stakeholder (financial, reputation etc) if investment priorities does not go ahead or fails to deliver the objectives?
<--- Score

85. How can you incorporate support to ensure safe and effective use of investment priorities into the services that you provide?
<--- Score

86. What are the key enablers to make this investment priorities move?

<--- Score

87. What is something you believe that nearly no one agrees with you on?
<--- Score

88. What are your personal philosophies regarding investment priorities and how do they influence your work?
<--- Score

89. What stupid rule would you most like to kill?
<--- Score

90. If you weren't already in this business, would you enter it today? And if not, what are you going to do about it?
<--- Score

91. What is the overall talent health of your organization as a whole at senior levels, and for each organization reporting to a member of the Senior Leadership Team?
<--- Score

92. Are all key stakeholders present at all Structured Walkthroughs?
<--- Score

93. Do you feel that more should be done in the investment priorities area?
<--- Score

94. What happens at your organization when people fail?
<--- Score

95. How do you create buy-in?
<--- Score

96. What counts that you are not counting?
<--- Score

97. How do you lead with investment priorities in mind?
<--- Score

98. Do you have a flow diagram of what happens?
<--- Score

99. Is your strategy driving your strategy? Or is the way in which you allocate resources driving your strategy?
<--- Score

100. What are your most important goals for the strategic investment priorities objectives?
<--- Score

101. How do you provide a safe environment -physically and emotionally?
<--- Score

102. In retrospect, of the projects that you pulled the plug on, what percent do you wish had been allowed to keep going, and what percent do you wish had ended earlier?
<--- Score

103. At what moment would you think; Will I get fired?
<--- Score

104. Do you have enough freaky customers in your portfolio pushing you to the limit day in and day out?
<--- Score

105. What are the potential basics of investment priorities fraud?
<--- Score

106. Do you think you know, or do you know you know ?
<--- Score

107. What are you trying to prove to yourself, and how might it be hijacking your life and business success?
<--- Score

108. Where can you break convention?
<--- Score

109. Will there be any necessary staff changes (redundancies or new hires)?
<--- Score

110. What is an unauthorized commitment?
<--- Score

111. How can you become the company that would put you out of business?
<--- Score

112. Are you using a design thinking approach and integrating Innovation, investment priorities Experience, and Brand Value?
<--- Score

113. Is it economical; do you have the time and

money?
<--- Score

114. What was the last experiment you ran?
<--- Score

115. Can you maintain your growth without detracting from the factors that have contributed to your success?
<--- Score

116. What knowledge, skills and characteristics mark a good investment priorities project manager?
<--- Score

117. Which models, tools and techniques are necessary?
<--- Score

118. What are the success criteria that will indicate that investment priorities objectives have been met and the benefits delivered?
<--- Score

119. What does your signature ensure?
<--- Score

120. Operational - will it work?
<--- Score

121. How do you govern and fulfill your societal responsibilities?
<--- Score

122. Do you know what you are doing? And who do you call if you don't?

<--- Score

123. Think of your investment priorities project, what
are the main functions?
<--- Score

124. What role does communication play in the
success or failure of a investment priorities project?
<--- Score

125. Are you / should you be revolutionary or
evolutionary?
<--- Score

126. What would have to be true for the option on the
table to be the best possible choice?
<--- Score

127. Is there any existing investment priorities
governance structure?
<--- Score

128. How do you determine the key elements that
affect investment priorities workforce satisfaction,
how are these elements determined for different
workforce groups and segments?
<--- Score

129. What business benefits will investment priorities
goals deliver if achieved?
<--- Score

130. How will you insure seamless interoperability of
investment priorities moving forward?
<--- Score

131. Who, on the executive team or the board, has spoken to a customer recently?
<--- Score

132. How do senior leaders deploy your organizations vision and values through your leadership system, to the workforce, to key suppliers and partners, and to customers and other stakeholders, as appropriate?
<--- Score

133. Do you have past investment priorities successes?
<--- Score

134. Who have you, as a company, historically been when you've been at your best?
<--- Score

135. Whom among your colleagues do you trust, and for what?
<--- Score

136. How much contingency will be available in the budget?
<--- Score

137. What could happen if you do not do it?
<--- Score

138. If your company went out of business tomorrow, would anyone who doesn't get a paycheck here care?
<--- Score

139. What potential megatrends could make your business model obsolete?
<--- Score

140. Why should people listen to you?
<--- Score

141. What are the gaps in your knowledge and experience?
<--- Score

142. How will you motivate the stakeholders with the least vested interest?
<--- Score

143. Do you see more potential in people than they do in themselves?
<--- Score

144. Instead of going to current contacts for new ideas, what if you reconnected with dormant contacts--the people you used to know? If you were going reactivate a dormant tie, who would it be?
<--- Score

145. How do you keep the momentum going?
<--- Score

146. If no one would ever find out about your accomplishments, how would you lead differently?
<--- Score

147. What are strategies for increasing support and reducing opposition?
<--- Score

148. What have you done to protect your business from competitive encroachment?
<--- Score

149. Is maximizing investment priorities protection the same as minimizing investment priorities loss?
<--- Score

150. Who are four people whose careers you have enhanced?
<--- Score

151. What is your formula for success in investment priorities ?
<--- Score

152. What happens when a new employee joins the organization?
<--- Score

153. Did your employees make progress today?
<--- Score

154. How do you make it meaningful in connecting investment priorities with what users do day-to-day?
<--- Score

155. Why is it important to have senior management support for a investment priorities project?
<--- Score

156. What is your BATNA (best alternative to a negotiated agreement)?
<--- Score

157. What is the craziest thing you can do?
<--- Score

158. Who are your customers?

<--- Score

159. If you do not follow, then how to lead?
<--- Score

160. What are the challenges?
<--- Score

161. In a project to restructure investment priorities outcomes, which stakeholders would you involve?
<--- Score

162. How do you manage investment priorities Knowledge Management (KM)?
<--- Score

163. What is the funding source for this project?
<--- Score

164. Which individuals, teams or departments will be involved in investment priorities?
<--- Score

165. What is the estimated value of the project?
<--- Score

166. If you were responsible for initiating and implementing major changes in your organization, what steps might you take to ensure acceptance of those changes?
<--- Score

167. How do you ensure that implementations of investment priorities products are done in a way that ensures safety?
<--- Score

168. Political -is anyone trying to undermine this project?
<--- Score

169. Why is investment priorities important for you now?
<--- Score

170. Can the schedule be done in the given time?
<--- Score

171. Do you have the right people on the bus?
<--- Score

172. How do you track customer value, profitability or financial return, organizational success, and sustainability?
<--- Score

173. Who will provide the final approval of investment priorities deliverables?
<--- Score

174. How likely is it that a customer would recommend your company to a friend or colleague?
<--- Score

175. Is the investment priorities organization completing tasks effectively and efficiently?
<--- Score

176. Ask yourself: how would you do this work if you only had one staff member to do it?
<--- Score

177. Will it be accepted by users?
<--- Score

178. How do you listen to customers to obtain actionable information?
<--- Score

179. What is the range of capabilities?
<--- Score

180. Who will determine interim and final deadlines?
<--- Score

181. What are the essentials of internal investment priorities management?
<--- Score

182. What management system can you use to leverage the investment priorities experience, ideas, and concerns of the people closest to the work to be done?
<--- Score

183. Who uses your product in ways you never expected?
<--- Score

184. What is the source of the strategies for investment priorities strengthening and reform?
<--- Score

185. Who is responsible for errors?
<--- Score

186. Are the criteria for selecting recommendations stated?

<--- Score

187. Are assumptions made in investment priorities stated explicitly?
<--- Score

188. How long will it take to change?
<--- Score

189. Who is on the team?
<--- Score

190. What is the kind of project structure that would be appropriate for your investment priorities project, should it be formal and complex, or can it be less formal and relatively simple?
<--- Score

191. How important is investment priorities to the user organizations mission?
<--- Score

192. What trophy do you want on your mantle?
<--- Score

193. What are internal and external investment priorities relations?
<--- Score

194. Who is the main stakeholder, with ultimate responsibility for driving investment priorities forward?
<--- Score

195. How do you deal with investment priorities changes?

<--- Score

Add up total points for this section:
_____ = Total points for this section

Divided by: _____ (number of
statements answered) = _____
Average score for this section

Transfer your score to the investment
priorities Index at the beginning of the
Self-Assessment.

Investment Priorities and Managing Projects, Criteria for Project Managers:

1.0 Initiating Process Group: Investment Priorities

1. At which cmmi level are software processes documented, standardized, and integrated into a standard to-be practiced process for your organization?

2. If action is called for, what form should it take?

3. Are you just doing busywork to pass the time?

4. What are the pressing issues of the hour?

5. Have the stakeholders identified all individual requirements pertaining to business process?

6. Did the Investment Priorities project team have the right skills?

7. How can you make your needs known?

8. Does the Investment Priorities project team have enough people to execute the Investment Priorities project plan?

9. Who is behind the Investment Priorities project?

10. What were things that you did well, and could improve, and how?

11. How well defined and documented were the Investment Priorities project management processes you chose to use?

12. Were decisions made in a timely manner?

13. Do you know if the Investment Priorities project requires outside equipment or vendor resources?

14. What do they need to know about the Investment Priorities project?

15. The Investment Priorities project you are managing has nine stakeholders. How many channel of communications are there between corresponding stakeholders?

16. Have requirements been tested, approved, and fulfill the Investment Priorities project scope?

17. Are identified risks being monitored properly, are new risks arising during the Investment Priorities project or are foreseen risks occurring?

18. What will you do?

19. How well did the chosen processes produce the expected results?

20. How will you do it?

1.1 Project Charter: Investment Priorities

21. When is a charter needed?

22. Major high-level milestone targets: what events measure progress?

23. What are the known stakeholder requirements?

24. Why do you need to manage scope?

25. Investment Priorities project background: what is the primary motivation for this Investment Priorities project?

26. When do you use a Investment Priorities project Charter?

27. Dependent Investment Priorities projects: what Investment Priorities projects must be underway or completed before this Investment Priorities project can be successful?

28. What are the constraints?

29. What is the business need?

30. Fit with other Products Compliments – Cannibalizes?

31. How will you know that a change is an improvement?

32. Are there special technology requirements?

33. Why have you chosen the aim you have set forth?

34. Run it as as a startup?

35. What are some examples of a business case?

36. What metrics could you look at?

37. Success determination factors: how will the success of the Investment Priorities project be determined from the customers perspective?

38. What date will the task finish?

39. Who ise input and support will this Investment Priorities project require?

40. Who manages integration?

1.2 Stakeholder Register: Investment Priorities

41. What is the power of the stakeholder?

42. How big is the gap?

43. What are the major Investment Priorities project milestones requiring communications or providing communications opportunities?

44. Is your organization ready for change?

45. Who is managing stakeholder engagement?

46. How much influence do they have on the Investment Priorities project?

47. What & Why?

48. Who are the stakeholders?

49. What opportunities exist to provide communications?

50. How will reports be created?

51. How should employers make voices heard?

52. Who wants to talk about Security?

1.3 Stakeholder Analysis Matrix: Investment Priorities

53. Location and geographical?

54. Which conditions out of the control of the management are crucial to contribute for the achievement of the development objective?

55. Effects on core activities, distraction?

56. Opponents; who are the opponents?

57. Beneficiaries; who are the potential beneficiaries?

58. Technology development and innovation?

59. What are the mechanisms of public and social accountability, and how can they be made better?

60. Market developments?

61. Information and research?

62. How can you fill the need to show progress?

63. Who will be affected by the work?

64. Accreditations, qualifications, certifications?

65. Who is most interested in information about the topic and/or has previously initiated interest?

66. What tools would help you communicate?

67. Are the interests in line with the program objectives?

68. What makes a person a stakeholder?

69. Will the impacts be local, national or international?

70. Who is directly responsible for decisions on issues important to the Investment Priorities project?

71. Cultural, attitudinal, behavioural?

72. Contributions to policy and practice?

2.0 Planning Process Group: Investment Priorities

73. When will the Investment Priorities project be done?

74. On which process should team members spend the most time?

75. Will you be replaced?

76. Product breakdown structure (pbs): what is the Investment Priorities project result or product, and how should it look like, what are its parts?

77. What is the NEXT thing to do?

78. Is the Investment Priorities project making progress in helping to achieve the set results?

79. How are the principles of aid effectiveness (ownership, alignment, management for development results and mutual responsibility) being applied in the Investment Priorities project?

80. Have more efficient (sensitive) and appropriate measures been adopted to respond to the political and socio-cultural problems identified?

81. To what extent are the visions and actions of the partners consistent or divergent with regard to the program?

82. Is the pace of implementing the products of the program ensuring the completeness of the results of the Investment Priorities project?

83. How do you integrate Investment Priorities project Planning with the Iterative/Evolutionary SDLC?

84. How well defined and documented are the Investment Priorities project management processes you chose to use?

85. Is the Investment Priorities project supported by national and/or local organizations?

86. How well do the team follow the chosen processes?

87. To what extent are the participating departments coordinating with each other?

88. Is the duration of the program sufficient to ensure a cycle that will Investment Priorities project the sustainability of the interventions?

89. What is the difference between the early schedule and late schedule?

90. If task x starts two days late, what is the effect on the Investment Priorities project end date?

91. When developing the estimates for Investment Priorities project phases, you choose to add the individual estimates for the activities that comprise each phase. What type of estimation method are you using?

92. If you are late, will anybody notice?

2.1 Project Management Plan: Investment Priorities

93. How well are you able to manage your risk?

94. Are comparable cost estimates used for comparing, screening and selecting alternative plans, and has a reasonable cost estimate been developed for the recommended plan?

95. What is risk management?

96. What would you do differently what did not work?

97. What are the deliverables?

98. What data/reports/tools/etc. do program managers need?

99. How do you manage integration?

100. What went right?

101. Do there need to be organizational changes?

102. Is mitigation authorized or recommended?

103. Are calculations and results of analyzes essentially correct?

104. Is the budget realistic?

105. What are the training needs?

106. What if, for example, the positive direction and vision of your organization causes expected trends to change resulting in greater need than expected?

107. What goes into your Investment Priorities project Charter?

108. Who is the sponsor?

109. Do the proposed changes from the Investment Priorities project include any significant risks to safety?

110. Does the implementation plan have an appropriate division of responsibilities?

111. Has the selected plan been formulated using cost effectiveness and incremental analysis techniques?

2.2 Scope Management Plan: Investment Priorities

112. Is there an issues management plan in place?

113. For which criterion is it tolerable not to meet the original parameters?

114. What are the risks that could significantly affect the resources needed for the Investment Priorities project?

115. Are procurement deliverables arriving on time and to specification?

116. Is each item clearly and completely defined?

117. Do you have the reasons why the changes to your organizational systems and capabilities are required?

118. Are the existing and future without-plan conditions reasonable and appropriate?

119. Are tasks tracked by hours?

120. What are the risks that could significantly affect the budget of the Investment Priorities project?

121. Are the results of quality assurance reviews provided to affected groups & individuals?

122. Are agendas created for each meeting with

meeting objectives, meeting topics, invitee list, and action items from past meetings?

123. When will scope verification be performed?

124. Have Investment Priorities project management standards and procedures been identified / established and documented?

125. Who is responsible for monitoring the Investment Priorities project scope to ensure the Investment Priorities project remains within the scope baseline?

126. Have reserves been created to address risks?

127. Is a pmo (Investment Priorities project management office) in place and provide oversight to the Investment Priorities project?

128. Has process improvement efforts been completed before requirements efforts begin?

129. Are corrective actions taken when actual results are substantially different from detailed Investment Priorities project plan (variances)?

130. Are the budget estimates reasonable?

131. Describe how the deliverables will be verified against the Investment Priorities project scope. To whom will the deliverables be first presented for inspection and verification?

2.3 Requirements Management Plan: Investment Priorities

132. Do you have an appropriate arrangement for meetings?

133. Does the Investment Priorities project have a Change Control process?

134. Do you have price sheets and a methodology for determining the total proposal cost?

135. How will you communicate scheduled tasks to other team members?

136. Is requirements work dependent on any other specific Investment Priorities project or non-Investment Priorities project activities (e.g. funding, approvals, procurement)?

137. When and how will a requirements baseline be established in this Investment Priorities project?

138. Did you use declarative statements?

139. How knowledgeable is the team in the proposed application area?

140. Will you perform a Requirements Risk assessment and develop a plan to deal with risks?

141. If it exists, where is it housed?

142. Are all the stakeholders ready for the transition into the user community?

143. Will the contractors involved take full responsibility?

144. To see if a requirement statement is sufficiently well-defined, read it from the developers perspective. Mentally add the phrase, call me when youre done to the end of the requirement and see if that makes you nervous. In other words, would you need additional clarification from the author to understand the requirement well enough to design and implement it?

145. In case of software development; Should you have a test for each code module?

146. Do you know which stakeholders will participate in the requirements effort?

147. Is any organizational data being used or stored?

148. How detailed should the Investment Priorities project get?

149. How will the information be distributed?

150. Is there formal agreement on who has authority to request a change in requirements?

151. What are you counting on?

2.4 Requirements Documentation: Investment Priorities

152. What are the potential disadvantages/ advantages?

153. What can tools do for us?

154. Is new technology needed?

155. How linear / iterative is your Requirements Gathering process (or will it be)?

156. What marketing channels do you want to use: e-mail, letter or sms?

157. Do technical resources exist?

158. What is your Elevator Speech?

159. How do you get the user to tell you what they want?

160. Can the requirements be checked?

161. How does the proposed Investment Priorities project contribute to the overall objectives of your organization?

162. How will requirements be documented and who signs off on them?

163. Has requirements gathering uncovered

information that would necessitate changes?

164. How much does requirements engineering cost?

165. Is the requirement realistically testable?

166. Do your constraints stand?

167. Who is interacting with the system?

168. Have the benefits identified with the system being identified clearly?

169. Are all functions required by the customer included?

170. Where are business rules being captured?

171. What is a show stopper in the requirements?

2.5 Requirements Traceability Matrix: Investment Priorities

172. Describe the process for approving requirements so they can be added to the traceability matrix and Investment Priorities project work can be performed. Will the Investment Priorities project requirements become approved in writing?

173. What is the WBS?

174. Will you use a Requirements Traceability Matrix?

175. How small is small enough?

176. How do you manage scope?

177. Why do you manage scope?

178. Why use a WBS?

179. What percentage of Investment Priorities projects are producing traceability matrices between requirements and other work products?

180. How will it affect the stakeholders personally in career?

181. Do you have a clear understanding of all subcontracts in place?

182. What are the chronologies, contingencies, consequences, criteria?

183. Is there a requirements traceability process in place?

2.6 Project Scope Statement: Investment Priorities

184. Are the meetings set up to have assigned note takers that will add action/issues to the issue list?

185. Have you been able to easily identify success criteria and create objective measurements for each of the Investment Priorities project scopes goal statements?

186. What are the major deliverables of the Investment Priorities project?

187. Who will you recommend approve the change, and when do you recommend the change reviews occur?

188. Is an issue management process documented and filed?

189. Is the plan for your organization of the Investment Priorities project resources adequate?

190. Investment Priorities project lead, team lead, solution architect?

191. Has a method and process for requirement tracking been developed?

192. Will this process be communicated to the customer and Investment Priorities project team?

193. Risks?

194. Change management vs. change leadership - what is the difference?

195. Is there a Quality Assurance Plan documented and filed?

196. Are there specific processes you will use to evaluate and approve/reject changes?

197. Will the risk status be reported to management on a regular and frequent basis?

198. Were key Investment Priorities project stakeholders brought into the Investment Priorities project Plan?

199. Do you anticipate new stakeholders joining the Investment Priorities project over time?

200. Elements of scope management that deal with concept development ?

201. Have you been able to thoroughly document the Investment Priorities projects assumptions and constraints?

202. If you were to write a list of what should not be included in the scope statement, what are the things that you would recommend be described as out-of-scope?

203. Are there completion/verification criteria defined for each task producing an output?

2.7 Assumption and Constraint Log: Investment Priorities

204. If it is out of compliance, should the process be amended or should the Plan be amended?

205. Are best practices and metrics employed to identify issues, progress, performance, etc.?

206. Is this process still needed?

207. Contradictory information between different documents?

208. Are there processes in place to ensure that all the terms and code concepts have been documented consistently?

209. Are there cosmetic errors that hinder readability and comprehension?

210. Are there processes in place to ensure internal consistency between the source code components?

211. Have the scope, objectives, costs, benefits and impacts been communicated to all involved and/or impacted stakeholders and work groups?

212. What would you gain if you spent time working to improve this process?

213. What strengths do you have?

214. How can you prevent/fix violations?

215. Is the amount of effort justified by the anticipated value of forming a new process?

216. Are there procedures in place to effectively manage interdependencies with other Investment Priorities projects / systems?

217. Security analysis has access to information that is sanitized?

218. Are there ways to reduce the time it takes to get something approved?

219. Were the system requirements formally reviewed prior to initiating the design phase?

220. How many Investment Priorities project staff does this specific process affect?

221. Does the traceability documentation describe the tool and/or mechanism to be used to capture traceability throughout the life cycle?

222. Do you know what your customers expectations are regarding this process?

223. What weaknesses do you have?

2.8 Work Breakdown Structure: Investment Priorities

224. When do you stop?

225. Why is it useful?

226. How will you and your Investment Priorities project team define the Investment Priorities projects scope and work breakdown structure?

227. Is the work breakdown structure (wbs) defined and is the scope of the Investment Priorities project clear with assigned deliverable owners?

228. How much detail?

229. When does it have to be done?

230. Who has to do it?

231. What is the probability of completing the Investment Priorities project in less that xx days?

232. How far down?

233. Why would you develop a Work Breakdown Structure?

234. Where does it take place?

235. Is it still viable?

236. What is the probability that the Investment Priorities project duration will exceed xx weeks?

237. Do you need another level?

238. Is it a change in scope?

239. How big is a work-package?

2.9 WBS Dictionary: Investment Priorities

240. What went wrong?

241. Are significant decision points, constraints, and interfaces identified as key milestones?

242. Incurrence of actual indirect costs in excess of budgets, by element of expense?

243. Are authorized changes being incorporated in a timely manner?

244. Is data disseminated to the contractors management timely, accurate, and usable?

245. Are budgets or values assigned to work packages and planning packages in terms of dollars, hours, or other measurable units?

246. Are work packages reasonably short in time duration or do they have adequate objective indicators/milestones to minimize subjectivity of the in process work evaluation?

247. Is the anticipated (firm and potential) business base Investment Priorities projected in a rational, consistent manner?

248. Are overhead cost budgets established for each organization which has authority to incur overhead costs?

249. Are records maintained to show full accountability for all material purchased for the contract, including the residual inventory?

250. Does the contractors system provide for accurate cost accumulation and assignment to control accounts in a manner consistent with the budgets using recognized acceptable costing techniques?

251. Is all budget available as management reserve identified and excluded from the performance measurement baseline?

252. Does the contractors system provide for the determination of cost variances attributable to the excess usage of material?

253. Is all contract work included in the CWBS?

254. Are overhead budgets and costs being handled according to the disclosure statement when applicable, or otherwise properly classified (for example, engineering overhead, IR&D)?

255. Are estimates of costs at completion generated in a rational, consistent manner?

256. The wbs is developed as part of a joint planning session. and how do you know that youhave done this right?

257. Time-phased control account budgets?

258. Are the procedures for identifying indirect costs to incurring organizations, indirect cost pools, and

allocating the costs from the pools to the contracts formally documented?

259. Does the cost accumulation system provide for summarization of indirect costs from the point of allocation to the contract total?

2.10 Schedule Management Plan: Investment Priorities

260. Is an industry recognized mechanized support tool(s) being used for Investment Priorities project scheduling & tracking?

261. Are risk triggers captured?

262. Were Investment Priorities project team members involved in detailed estimating and scheduling?

263. Are the quality tools and methods identified in the Quality Plan appropriate to the Investment Priorities project?

264. What will be the format of the schedule model?

265. Will rolling way planning be used?

266. Is the development plan and/or process documented?

267. Time for overtime?

268. Is there a set of procedures defining the scope, procedures, and deliverables defining quality control?

269. Are the processes for schedule assessment and analysis defined?

270. Was the scope definition used in task sequencing?

271. Were the budget estimates reasonable?

272. Is documentation created for communication with the suppliers and Vendors?

273. Who is responsible for estimating the activity durations?

274. Does a documented Investment Priorities project organizational policy & plan (i.e. governance model) exist?

275. Are actuals compared against estimates to analyze and correct variances?

276. Are there any activities or deliverables being added or gold-plated that could be dropped or scaled back without falling short of the original requirement?

277. Is there a requirements change management processes in place?

278. Are meeting objectives identified for each meeting?

2.11 Activity List: Investment Priorities

279. What are the critical bottleneck activities?

280. Who will perform the work?

281. Are the required resources available or need to be acquired?

282. How can the Investment Priorities project be displayed graphically to better visualize the activities?

283. How much slack is available in the Investment Priorities project?

284. How detailed should a Investment Priorities project get?

285. For other activities, how much delay can be tolerated?

286. What went well?

287. What is your organizations history in doing similar activities?

288. What is the total time required to complete the Investment Priorities project if no delays occur?

289. When will the work be performed?

290. What did not go as well?

291. Should you include sub-activities?

292. How will it be performed?

293. Can you determine the activity that must finish, before this activity can start?

294. What is the probability the Investment Priorities project can be completed in xx weeks?

295. How should ongoing costs be monitored to try to keep the Investment Priorities project within budget?

2.12 Activity Attributes: Investment Priorities

296. Is there a trend during the year?

297. Are the required resources available?

298. What is the general pattern here?

299. What is missing?

300. Do you feel very comfortable with your prediction?

301. Were there other ways you could have organized the data to achieve similar results?

302. How many days do you need to complete the work scope with a limit of X number of resources?

303. Resource is assigned to?

304. How difficult will it be to complete specific activities on this Investment Priorities project?

305. How much activity detail is required?

306. Have you identified the Activity Leveling Priority code value on each activity?

307. Can more resources be added?

308. What activity do you think you should spend the

most time on?

309. Activity: what is Missing?

310. Where else does it apply?

311. Would you consider either of corresponding activities an outlier?

312. Have constraints been applied to the start and finish milestones for the phases?

2.13 Milestone List: Investment Priorities

313. Sustainable financial backing?

314. Competitive advantages?

315. Describe the concept of the technology, product or service that will be or has been developed. How will it be used?

316. Usps (unique selling points)?

317. What specific improvements did you make to the Investment Priorities project proposal since the previous time?

318. Can you derive how soon can the whole Investment Priorities project finish?

319. What background experience, skills, and strengths does the team bring to your organization?

320. Vital contracts and partners?

321. How soon can the activity start?

322. How difficult will it be to do specific activities on this Investment Priorities project?

323. Identify critical paths (one or more) and which activities are on the critical path?

324. Obstacles faced?

325. Reliability of data, plan predictability?

326. Environmental effects?

327. How will the milestone be verified?

328. Insurmountable weaknesses?

329. Who will manage the Investment Priorities project on a day-to-day basis?

330. Loss of key staff?

331. Calculate how long can activity be delayed?

2.14 Network Diagram: Investment Priorities

332. Where do schedules come from?

333. Exercise: what is the probability that the Investment Priorities project duration will exceed xx weeks?

334. What can be done concurrently?

335. Will crashing x weeks return more in benefits than it costs?

336. What is the probability of completing the Investment Priorities project in less that xx days?

337. What to do and When?

338. What is the completion time?

339. What job or jobs could run concurrently?

340. Are you on time?

341. Planning: who, how long, what to do?

342. Where do you schedule uncertainty time?

343. What are the Key Success Factors?

344. What activities must occur simultaneously with this activity?

345. What controls the start and finish of a job?

346. If x is long, what would be the completion time if you break x into two parallel parts of y weeks and z weeks?

347. Can you calculate the confidence level?

348. What is the lowest cost to complete this Investment Priorities project in xx weeks?

349. How difficult will it be to do specific activities on this Investment Priorities project?

350. What must be completed before an activity can be started?

2.15 Activity Resource Requirements: Investment Priorities

351. Organizational Applicability?

352. When does monitoring begin?

353. What are constraints that you might find during the Human Resource Planning process?

354. Why do you do that?

355. How do you handle petty cash?

356. What is the Work Plan Standard?

357. Is there anything planned that does not need to be here?

358. How many signatures do you require on a check and does this match what is in your policy and procedures?

359. Anything else?

360. Which logical relationship does the PDM use most often?

361. Other support in specific areas?

362. Are there unresolved issues that need to be addressed?

363. Do you use tools like decomposition and rolling-wave planning to produce the activity list and other outputs?

364. How do you manage time?

2.16 Resource Breakdown Structure: Investment Priorities

365. Why do you do it?

366. Who needs what information?

367. What can you do to improve productivity?

368. Who is allowed to perform which functions?

369. Why is this important?

370. Changes based on input from stakeholders?

371. Who delivers the information?

372. What is Investment Priorities project communication management?

373. Why time management?

374. What are the requirements for resource data?

375. What defines a successful Investment Priorities project?

376. What defines a successful Investment Priorities project?

377. Who will use the system?

378. Which resource planning tool provides

information on resource responsibility and accountability?

379. Any changes from stakeholders?

380. Is predictive resource analysis being done?

2.17 Activity Duration Estimates: Investment Priorities

381. Do procedures exist that identify when and how human resources are introduced and removed from the Investment Priorities project?

382. What questions do you have about the sample documents provided?

383. What do you think about the WBSs for them?

384. Are adjustments implemented to correct or prevent defects?

385. What tasks must precede this task?

386. Does a procedure exist to ensure the Investment Priorities project work is completed in the appropriate sequence and on time?

387. What type of information goes in a quality assurance plan?

388. Write a oneto two-page paper describing your dream team for this Investment Priorities project. What type of people would you want on your team?

389. How does a Investment Priorities project life cycle differ from a product life cycle?

390. Do scope statements include the Investment Priorities project objectives and expected

deliverables?

391. Calculate the expected duration for an activity that has a most likely time of 3, a pessimistic time of 10, and a optimiztic time of 2?

392. Does a process exist to determine the probability of risk events?

393. What are key inputs and outputs of the software?

394. How does Investment Priorities project management relate to other disciplines?

395. Investment Priorities project has three critical paths. Which BEST describes how this affects the Investment Priorities project?

396. What is the duration of the critical path for this Investment Priorities project?

397. Briefly summarize the work done by Maslow, Herzberg, McClellan, McGregor, Ouchi, Thamhain and Wilemon, and Covey. How do theories relate to Investment Priorities project management?

398. How could you use each technique in your organization?

2.18 Duration Estimating Worksheet: Investment Priorities

399. How can the Investment Priorities project be displayed graphically to better visualize the activities?

400. Is a construction detail attached (to aid in explanation)?

401. What is an Average Investment Priorities project?

402. What questions do you have?

403. Does the Investment Priorities project provide innovative ways for stakeholders to overcome obstacles or deliver better outcomes?

404. Is this operation cost effective?

405. What info is needed?

406. What work will be included in the Investment Priorities project?

407. What utility impacts are there?

408. What is your role?

409. Do any colleagues have experience with your organization and/or RFPs?

410. What is cost and Investment Priorities project cost management?

411. How should ongoing costs be monitored to try to keep the Investment Priorities project within budget?

412. What is next?

413. When does your organization expect to be able to complete it?

414. Can the Investment Priorities project be constructed as planned?

415. Define the work as completely as possible. What work will be included in the Investment Priorities project?

2.19 Project Schedule: Investment Priorities

416. To what degree is do you feel the entire team was committed to the Investment Priorities project schedule?

417. If you can not fix it, how do you do it differently?

418. What is risk?

419. How do you use schedules?

420. Is the Investment Priorities project schedule available for all Investment Priorities project team members to review?

421. Are key risk mitigation strategies added to the Investment Priorities project schedule?

422. Why is software Investment Priorities project disaster so common?

423. Is Investment Priorities project work proceeding in accordance with the original Investment Priorities project schedule?

424. How much slack is available in the Investment Priorities project?

425. Change management required?

426. Are quality inspections and review activities

listed in the Investment Priorities project schedule(s)?

427. How can you shorten the schedule?

428. Master Investment Priorities project schedule?

2.20 Cost Management Plan: Investment Priorities

429. Escalation criteria met?

430. What are the nine areas of expertise?

431. Is a stakeholder management plan in place that covers topics?

432. Are all vendor contracts closed out?

433. Were Investment Priorities project team members involved in the development of activity & task decomposition?

434. Has your organization readiness assessment been conducted?

435. Are there checklists created to determine if all quality processes are followed?

436. Are vendor invoices audited for accuracy before payment?

437. Are changes in deliverable commitments agreed to by all affected groups & individuals?

438. What is cost and Investment Priorities project cost management?

439. Are the key elements of a Investment Priorities project Charter present?

440. Has a quality assurance plan been developed for the Investment Priorities project?

441. Are internal Investment Priorities project status meetings held at reasonable intervals?

442. Exclusions – is there scope to be performed or provided by others?

443. Cost variances – how will cost variances be identified and corrected?

444. Are status reports received per the Investment Priorities project Plan?

445. Who will prepare the cost estimates?

446. Is it possible to track all classes of Investment Priorities project work (e.g. scheduled, un-scheduled, defect repair, etc.)?

447. Are non-critical path items updated and agreed upon with the teams?

2.21 Activity Cost Estimates: Investment Priorities

448. What areas were overlooked on this Investment Priorities project?

449. Does the activity serve a common type of customer?

450. Review – what are some common errors in activities to avoid?

451. What is a Investment Priorities project Management Plan?

452. Is costing method consistent with study goals?

453. In which phase of the acquisition process cycle does source qualifications reside?

454. How do you treat administrative costs in the activity inventory?

455. Did the Investment Priorities project team have the right skills?

456. What is the Investment Priorities projects sustainability strategy that will ensure Investment Priorities project results will endure or be sustained?

457. Why do you manage cost?

458. Does the activity use a common approach or

business function to deliver its results?

459. How Award?

460. What is the last item a Investment Priorities project manager must do to finalize Investment Priorities project close-out?

461. Does the estimator have experience?

462. What is included in indirect cost being allocated?

463. Who determines the quality and expertise of contractors?

464. What are the audit requirements?

465. What defines a successful Investment Priorities project?

2.22 Cost Estimating Worksheet: Investment Priorities

466. What can be included?

467. Identify the timeframe necessary to monitor progress and collect data to determine how the selected measure has changed?

468. Can a trend be established from historical performance data on the selected measure and are the criteria for using trend analysis or forecasting methods met?

469. What will others want?

470. Value pocket identification & quantification what are value pockets?

471. Is it feasible to establish a control group arrangement?

472. Ask: are others positioned to know, are others credible, and will others cooperate?

473. Who is best positioned to know and assist in identifying corresponding factors?

474. Will the Investment Priorities project collaborate with the local community and leverage resources?

475. What is the estimated labor cost today based upon this information?

476. What is the purpose of estimating?

477. What additional Investment Priorities project(s) could be initiated as a result of this Investment Priorities project?

478. What costs are to be estimated?

479. Is the Investment Priorities project responsive to community need?

480. What happens to any remaining funds not used?

481. How will the results be shared and to whom?

482. Does the Investment Priorities project provide innovative ways for stakeholders to overcome obstacles or deliver better outcomes?

2.23 Cost Baseline: Investment Priorities

483. How fast?

484. Have the resources used by the Investment Priorities project been reassigned to other units or Investment Priorities projects?

485. Is request in line with priorities?

486. Is there anything unique in this Investment Priorities projects scope statement that will affect resources?

487. Has the documentation relating to operation and maintenance of the product(s) or service(s) been delivered to, and accepted by, operations management?

488. On budget?

489. Has training and knowledge transfer of the operations organization been completed?

490. Is the cr within Investment Priorities project scope?

491. Is the requested change request a result of changes in other Investment Priorities project(s)?

492. Does the suggested change request represent a desired enhancement to the products functionality?

493. What is it ?

494. How will cost estimates be used?

495. What is your organizations history in doing similar tasks?

496. Does a process exist for establishing a cost baseline to measure Investment Priorities project performance?

497. On time?

498. Has the Investment Priorities projected annual cost to operate and maintain the product(s) or service(s) been approved and funded?

499. Have the lessons learned been filed with the Investment Priorities project Management Office?

500. Have all approved changes to the cost baseline been identified and impact on the Investment Priorities project documented?

2.24 Quality Management Plan: Investment Priorities

501. Modifications to the requirements?

502. Are there trends or hot spots?

503. Results Available?

504. Checking the completeness and appropriateness of the sampling and testing. Were the right locations/samples tested for the right parameters?

505. Sampling part of task?

506. What is quality and how will you ensure it?

507. How are records kept in the office?

508. Documented results available?

509. What are the appropriate test methods to be used?

510. Does the program use other agents to collect samples?

511. Was trending evident between reviews?

512. Is there a Steering Committee in place?

513. How is staff trained on the recording of field notes?

514. How are calibration records kept?

515. With the five whys method, the team considers why the issue being explored occurred. do others then take that initial answer and ask why?

516. Who is responsible for approving the qapp?

517. Does a documented Investment Priorities project organizational policy & plan (i.e. governance model) exist?

518. Do you periodically review your data quality system to see that it is up to date and appropriate?

519. What are your organizations current levels and trends for the already stated measures related to customer satisfaction/ dissatisfaction and product/ service performance?

520. How will you know that a change is actually an improvement?

2.25 Quality Metrics: Investment Priorities

521. Are documents on hand to provide explanations of privacy and confidentiality?

522. Can visual measures help you to filter visualizations of interest?

523. How can the effectiveness of each of the activities be measured?

524. Did the team meet the Investment Priorities project success criteria documented in the Quality Metrics Matrix?

525. Is quality culture a competitive advantage?

526. What approved evidence based screening tools can be used?

527. What do you measure?

528. What is the benchmark?

529. Were number of defects identified?

530. Why is now the time for quality metrics?

531. Do you know how much profit a 10% decrease in waste would generate?

532. Has it met internal or external standards?

533. Do the operators focus on determining; is there anything you need to worry about?

534. How do you communicate results and findings to upper management?

535. Was review conducted per standard protocols?

536. Are interface issues coordinated?

537. How does one achieve stability?

538. Who is willing to lead?

539. What forces exist that would cause them to change?

540. What happens if you get an abnormal result?

2.26 Process Improvement Plan: Investment Priorities

541. Where do you want to be?

542. Are you making progress on the goals?

543. Where are you now?

544. What actions are needed to address the problems and achieve the goals?

545. What makes people good SPI coaches?

546. Have the frequency of collection and the points in the process where measurements will be made been determined?

547. Are you meeting the quality standards?

548. What personnel are the champions for the initiative?

549. How do you manage quality?

550. Are you following the quality standards?

551. The motive is determined by asking, Why do you want to achieve this goal?

552. Have the supporting tools been developed or acquired?

553. Modeling current processes is great, and will you ever see a return on that investment?

554. Why quality management?

555. What is the return on investment?

556. Purpose of goal: the motive is determined by asking, why do you want to achieve this goal?

557. Are there forms and procedures to collect and record the data?

558. If a process improvement framework is being used, which elements will help the problems and goals listed?

559. Does your process ensure quality?

560. What is the test-cycle concept?

2.27 Responsibility Assignment Matrix: Investment Priorities

561. Authorization to proceed with all authorized work?

562. Most people let you know when others re too busy, and are others really too busy?

563. What are the assigned resources?

564. If a role has only Signing-off, or only Communicating responsibility and has no Performing, Accountable, or Monitoring responsibility, is it necessary?

565. Ideas for developing soft skills at your organization?

566. What are the assumptions?

567. Are the bases and rates for allocating costs from each indirect pool consistently applied?

568. Are the wbs and organizational levels for application of the Investment Priorities projected overhead costs identified?

569. Too many rs: with too many people labeled as doing the work, are there too many hands involved?

570. Changes in the nature of the overhead requirements?

571. Are meaningful indicators identified for use in measuring the status of cost and schedule performance?

572. Not any rs, as, or cs: if an identified role is only informed, should others be eliminated from the matrix?

573. Too many is: do all the identified roles need to be routinely informed or only in exceptional circumstances?

574. When performing is split among two or more roles, is the work clearly defined so that the efforts are coordinated and the communication is clear?

575. Actual cost of work performed?

576. Are the overhead pools formally and adequately identified?

2.28 Roles and Responsibilities: Investment Priorities

577. Have you ever been a part of this team?

578. What should you do now to prepare yourself for a promotion, increased responsibilities or a different job?

579. Who is involved?

580. Is the data complete?

581. Does the team have access to and ability to use data analysis tools?

582. Attainable / achievable: the goal is attainable; can you actually accomplish the goal?

583. Are governance roles and responsibilities documented?

584. What expectations were met?

585. Accountabilities: what are the roles and responsibilities of individual team members?

586. Was the expectation clearly communicated?

587. Are your policies supportive of a culture of quality data?

588. Are Investment Priorities project team roles and

responsibilities identified and documented?

589. Once the responsibilities are defined for the Investment Priorities project, have the deliverables, roles and responsibilities been clearly communicated to every participant?

590. What is working well within your organizations performance management system?

591. Does your vision/mission support a culture of quality data?

592. Be specific; avoid generalities. Thank you and great work alone are insufficient. What exactly do you appreciate and why?

593. What should you do now to ensure that you are exceeding expectations and excelling in your current position?

594. Who is responsible for implementation activities and where will the functions, roles and responsibilities be defined?

595. Implementation of actions: Who are the responsible units?

596. What specific behaviors did you observe?

2.29 Human Resource Management Plan: Investment Priorities

597. What are the Staffing Requirements?

598. Are staff skills known and available for each task?

599. Has the schedule been baselined?

600. Do people have the competencies to meet the strategic objectives?

601. Are key risk mitigation strategies added to the Investment Priorities project schedule?

602. Were stakeholders aware and supportive of the principles and practices of modern cost estimation?

603. Are vendor contract reports, reviews and visits conducted periodically?

604. Were escalated issues resolved promptly?

605. Are target dates established for each milestone deliverable?

606. Is quality monitored from the perspective of the customers needs and expectations?

607. Specific - is the objective clear in terms of what, how, when, and where the situation will be changed?

608. Who are the people that make up your

organization and whom create the success that your organization enjoys as a whole?

609. How relevant is this attribute to this Investment Priorities project or audit?

610. Is an industry recognized support tool(s) being used for Investment Priorities project scheduling & tracking?

611. How do you determine what key skills and talents are needed to meet the objectives. Is your organization primarily focused on a specific industry?

612. Pareto diagrams, statistical sampling, flow charting or trend analysis used quality monitoring?

613. Does the Investment Priorities project have a Statement of Work?

2.30 Communications Management Plan: Investment Priorities

614. Who have you worked with in past, similar initiatives?

615. Do you have members of your team responsible for certain stakeholders?

616. Who did you turn to if you had questions?

617. Why do you manage communications?

618. Which team member will work with each stakeholder?

619. How will the person responsible for executing the communication item be notified?

620. What is Investment Priorities project communications management?

621. Will messages be directly related to the release strategy or phases of the Investment Priorities project?

622. Are there common objectives between the team and the stakeholder?

623. Do you ask; can you recommend others for you to talk with about this initiative?

624. What is the stakeholders level of authority?

625. Conflict resolution -which method when?

626. Are others needed?

627. Do you feel more overwhelmed by stakeholders?

628. Timing: when do the effects of the communication take place?

629. How is this initiative related to other portfolios, programs, or Investment Priorities projects?

630. Where do team members get information?

631. Do you prepare stakeholder engagement plans?

632. How were corresponding initiatives successful?

633. Are you constantly rushing from meeting to meeting?

2.31 Risk Management Plan: Investment Priorities

634. Have you worked with the customer in the past?

635. Was an original risk assessment/risk management plan completed?

636. What will the damage be?

637. How is risk monitoring performed?

638. Which is an input to the risk management process?

639. Is the customer technically sophisticated in the product area?

640. Who has experience with this?

641. Do the people have the right combinations of skills?

642. Is security a central objective?

643. Premium on reliability of product?

644. How much risk can you tolerate?

645. What is the likelihood?

646. Is the customer willing to establish rapid communication links with the developer?

647. For software; does the software interface with new or unproven hardware or unproven vendor products?

648. People risk -are people with appropriate skills available to help complete the Investment Priorities project?

649. What other risks are created by choosing an avoidance strategy?

650. Are Investment Priorities project requirements stable?

651. How will the Investment Priorities project know if your organizations risk response actions were effective?

652. Mitigation -how can you avoid the risk?

653. Are you on schedule?

2.32 Risk Register: Investment Priorities

654. What should you do now?

655. What are the assumptions and current status that support the assessment of the risk?

656. What would the impact to the Investment Priorities project objectives be should the risk arise?

657. What are your key risks/show istoppers and what is being done to manage them?

658. Are your objectives at risk?

659. What should the audit role be in establishing a risk management process?

660. Do you require further engagement?

661. What further options might be available for responding to the risk?

662. What evidence do you have to justify the likelihood score of the risk (audit, incident report, claim, complaints, inspection, internal review)?

663. What is the probability and impact of the risk occurring?

664. Who needs to know about this?

665. Schedule impact/severity estimated range (workdays) assume the event happens, what is the potential impact?

666. What is the reason for current performance gaps and do the risks and opportunities identified previously account for this?

667. User involvement: do you have the right users?

668. Can the likelihood and impact of failing to achieve corresponding recommendations and action plans be assessed?

669. Assume the event happens, what is the Most Likely impact?

670. Are there other alternative controls that could be implemented?

671. When would you develop a risk register?

672. What are the major risks facing the Investment Priorities project?

673. What can be done about it?

2.33 Probability and Impact Assessment: Investment Priorities

674. How risk averse are you?

675. How realistic is the timing of introduction?

676. Do you use diagramming techniques to show cause and effect?

677. Have top software and customer managers formally committed to support the Investment Priorities project?

678. What are the chances the event will occur?

679. What kind of preparation would be required to do this?

680. Is the present organizational structure for handling the Investment Priorities project sufficient?

681. Will there be an increase in the political conservatism?

682. What are the uncertainties associated with the technology selected for the Investment Priorities project?

683. Who should be responsible for the monitoring and tracking of the indicators youhave identified?

684. Are the software tools integrated with each

other?

685. What new technologies are being explored in the same area?

686. Which functions, departments, and activities of your organization are going to be affected?

687. What significant shift will occur in governmental policies, laws, and regulations pertaining to specific industries?

688. What is the Investment Priorities project managers level of commitment and professionalism?

689. Has something like this been done before?

690. How much risk do others need to take?

691. What risks are necessary to achieve success?

692. Do benefits and chances of success outweigh potential damage if success is not attained?

693. When and how will the recent breakthroughs in basic research lead to commercial products?

2.34 Probability and Impact Matrix: Investment Priorities

694. Is Investment Priorities project scope stable?

695. What will be the likely political situation during the life of the Investment Priorities project?

696. Who is going to be the consortium leader?

697. Do you have a mechanism for managing change?

698. Can it be enlarged by drawing people from other areas of your organization?

699. Are the risk data timely and relevant?

700. Have customers been involved fully in the definition of requirements?

701. Mandated delivery date?

702. Are Investment Priorities project requirements stable?

703. Are there alternative opinions/solutions/processes you should explore?

704. Are the best people available?

705. How are you working with risks?

706. What is your anticipated volatility of the

requirements?

707. What should be done with non-critical risks?

708. How are the local factors going to affect the absorption?

709. During which risk management process is a determination to transfer a risk made?

710. Does the Investment Priorities project team have experience with the technology to be implemented?

711. What are the current demands of the customer?

712. What are the uncertainties associated with the technology selected for the Investment Priorities project?

2.35 Risk Data Sheet: Investment Priorities

713. What can you do?

714. Has the most cost-effective solution been chosen?

715. What actions can be taken to eliminate or remove risk?

716. Who has a vested interest in how you perform as your organization (our stakeholders)?

717. Do effective diagnostic tests exist?

718. What if client refuses?

719. What will be the consequences if it happens?

720. What are you trying to achieve (Objectives)?

721. Type of risk identified?

722. What is the environment within which you operate (social trends, economic, community values, broad based participation, national directions etc.)?

723. What were the Causes that contributed?

724. What was measured?

725. What can happen?

726. What are you weak at and therefore need to do better?

727. Whom do you serve (customers)?

728. Are new hazards created?

729. Has a sensitivity analysis been carried out?

730. Potential for recurrence?

731. How do you handle product safely?

2.36 Procurement Management Plan: Investment Priorities

732. Has the business need been clearly defined?

733. What communication items need improvement?

734. What is the last item a Investment Priorities project manager must do to finalize Investment Priorities project close-out?

735. Are Investment Priorities project team roles and responsibilities identified and documented?

736. Are the quality tools and methods identified in the Quality Plan appropriate to the Investment Priorities project?

737. What types of contracts will be used?

738. Are assumptions being identified, recorded, analyzed, qualified and closed?

739. What is a Investment Priorities project Management Plan?

740. Have lessons learned been conducted after each Investment Priorities project release?

741. Sensitivity analysis?

742. Does the Investment Priorities project have a Quality Culture?

743. Have Investment Priorities project team accountabilities & responsibilities been clearly defined?

744. Is the communication plan being followed?

745. Staffing Requirements?

746. Have key stakeholders been identified?

747. Are cause and effect determined for risks when others occur?

748. Are meeting minutes captured and sent out after meetings?

2.37 Source Selection Criteria: Investment Priorities

749. What management structure does your organization consider as optimal for performing the contract?

750. What is the effect of the debriefing schedule on potential protests?

751. How do you ensure an integrated assessment of proposals?

752. Who is entitled to a debriefing?

753. What documentation is necessary regarding electronic communications?

754. Have all evaluators been trained?

755. Why promote competition?

756. Which contract type places the most risk on the seller?

757. What will you use to capture evaluation and subsequent documentation?

758. What evidence should be provided regarding proposal evaluations?

759. How do you encourage efficiency and consistency?

760. Is there collaboration among your evaluators?

761. Do proposed hours support content and schedule?

762. What should clarifications include?

763. How are clarifications and communications appropriately used?

764. What are the guiding principles for developing an evaluation report?

765. What is cost analysis and when should it be performed?

766. What source selection software is your team using?

767. When is it appropriate to conduct a preproposal conference?

768. What information may not be provided?

2.38 Stakeholder Management Plan: Investment Priorities

769. Is the quality assurance team identified?

770. After observing execution of process, is it in compliance with the documented Plan?

771. Are stakeholders aware and supportive of the principles and practices of modern software estimation?

772. Has the Investment Priorities project scope been baselined?

773. Are trade-offs between accepting the risk and mitigating the risk identified?

774. Are parking lot items captured?

775. Are Investment Priorities project contact logs kept up to date?

776. Have Investment Priorities project management standards and procedures been established and documented?

777. Has the Investment Priorities project manager been identified?

778. Why would you develop a Investment Priorities project Business Plan?

779. Are metrics used to evaluate and manage Vendors?

780. Have all stakeholders been identified?

781. Was trending evident between audits?

782. Are the Investment Priorities project team members located locally to the users/stakeholders?

783. Are the payment terms being followed?

784. Is the schedule updated on a periodic basis?

785. Are mitigation strategies identified?

786. Are the Investment Priorities project plans updated on a frequent basis?

787. Have the key elements of a coherent Investment Priorities project management strategy been established?

2.39 Change Management Plan: Investment Priorities

788. Who will fund the training?

789. Do you need new systems?

790. Will a different work structure focus people on what is important?

791. Who will be the change levers?

792. How might they respond to the message and if the response may be negative or open to misinterpretation, what else needs to be said?

793. Has the relevant business unit been notified of installation and support requirements?

794. What provokes organizational change?

795. How will the stakeholders share information and transfer knowledge?

796. What would be an estimate of the total cost for the activities required to carry out the change initiative?

797. What tasks are needed?

798. What policies and procedures need to be changed?

799. Clearly articulate the overall business benefits of the Investment Priorities project -why are you doing this now?

800. Have the systems been configured and tested?

801. Will the culture embrace or reject this change?

802. How will you deal with anger about the restricting of communications due to confidentiality considerations?

803. Do the proposed users have access to the appropriate documentation?

804. Would you need to tailor a special message for each segment of the audience?

805. How do you know the requirements you documented are the right ones?

3.0 Executing Process Group: Investment Priorities

806. Based on your Investment Priorities project communication management plan, what worked well?

807. What are the critical steps involved with strategy mapping?

808. Are the necessary foundations in place to ensure the sustainability of the results of the programme?

809. What is involved in the solicitation process?

810. Do the products created live up to the necessary quality?

811. When will the Investment Priorities project be done?

812. When is the appropriate time to bring the scorecard to Board meetings?

813. What is the difference between conceptual, application, and evaluative questions?

814. Measurable - are the targets measurable?

815. What is in place for ensuring adequate change control on Investment Priorities projects that involve outside contracts?

816. What is the product of your Investment Priorities project?

817. Contingency planning. if a risk event occurs, what will you do?

818. What are the main types of contracts if you do decide to outsource?

819. Will a new application be developed using existing hardware, software, and networks?

820. After how many days will the lease cost be the same as the purchase cost for the equipment?

821. How is Investment Priorities project performance information created and distributed?

822. What areas were overlooked on this Investment Priorities project?

823. Mitigate. what will you do to minimize the impact should a risk event occur?

824. What are deliverables of your Investment Priorities project?

3.1 Team Member Status Report: Investment Priorities

825. Are the attitudes of staff regarding Investment Priorities project work improving?

826. Are your organizations Investment Priorities projects more successful over time?

827. Why is it to be done?

828. When a teams productivity and success depend on collaboration and the efficient flow of information, what generally fails them?

829. Does your organization have the means (staff, money, contract, etc.) to produce or to acquire the product, good, or service?

830. How it is to be done?

831. Does the product, good, or service already exist within your organization?

832. Will the staff do training or is that done by a third party?

833. How can you make it practical?

834. Does every department have to have a Investment Priorities project Manager on staff?

835. Is there evidence that staff is taking a more

professional approach toward management of your organizations Investment Priorities projects?

836. Do you have an Enterprise Investment Priorities project Management Office (EPMO)?

837. What specific interest groups do you have in place?

838. What is to be done?

839. How does this product, good, or service meet the needs of the Investment Priorities project and your organization as a whole?

840. How much risk is involved?

841. How will resource planning be done?

842. The problem with Reward & Recognition Programs is that the truly deserving people all too often get left out. How can you make it practical?

843. Are the products of your organizations Investment Priorities projects meeting customers objectives?

3.2 Change Request: Investment Priorities

844. What is the change request log?

845. How is quality being addressed on the Investment Priorities project?

846. Who is responsible to authorize changes?

847. Customer acceptance plan how will the customer verify the change has been implemented successfully?

848. Why were your requested changes rejected or not made?

849. Does the schedule include Investment Priorities project management time and change request analysis time?

850. What is a Change Request Form?

851. Which requirements attributes affect the risk to reliability the most?

852. When do you create a change request?

853. Why do you want to have a change control system?

854. What are the basic mechanics of the Change Advisory Board (CAB)?

855. How shall the implementation of changes be recorded?

856. What can be filed?

857. Will the change use memory to the extent that other functions will be not have sufficient memory to operate effectively?

858. Have all related configuration items been properly updated?

859. What are the Impacts to your organization?

860. Will this change conflict with other requirements changes (e.g., lead to conflicting operational scenarios)?

861. Has the change been highlighted and documented in the CSCI?

862. Will all change requests be unconditionally tracked through this process?

863. Will new change requests be acknowledged in a timely manner?

3.3 Change Log: Investment Priorities

864. Is the submitted change a new change or a modification of a previously approved change?

865. Do the described changes impact on the integrity or security of the system?

866. Will the Investment Priorities project fail if the change request is not executed?

867. Is the change request open, closed or pending?

868. How does this relate to the standards developed for specific business processes?

869. Does the suggested change request seem to represent a necessary enhancement to the product?

870. Where do changes come from?

871. Is the requested change request a result of changes in other Investment Priorities project(s)?

872. Is the change request within Investment Priorities project scope?

873. When was the request submitted?

874. Who initiated the change request?

875. Is the change backward compatible without limitations?

876. Is this a mandatory replacement?

877. Should a more thorough impact analysis be conducted?

878. How does this change affect the timeline of the schedule?

879. How does this change affect scope?

880. When was the request approved?

3.4 Decision Log: Investment Priorities

881. What is your overall strategy for quality control / quality assurance procedures?

882. Behaviors; what are guidelines that the team has identified that will assist them with getting the most out of team meetings?

883. Decision-making process; how will the team make decisions?

884. How does the use a Decision Support System influence the strategies/tactics or costs?

885. How do you define success?

886. How do you know when you are achieving it?

887. At what point in time does loss become unacceptable?

888. How does provision of information, both in terms of content and presentation, influence acceptance of alternative strategies?

889. Which variables make a critical difference?

890. Meeting purpose; why does this team meet?

891. What was the rationale for the decision?

892. What eDiscovery problem or issue did your organization set out to fix or make better?

893. How consolidated and comprehensive a story can you tell by capturing currently available incident data in a central location and through a log of key decisions during an incident?

894. How does an increasing emphasis on cost containment influence the strategies and tactics used?

895. What is the average size of your matters in an applicable measurement?

896. Linked to original objective?

897. Does anything need to be adjusted?

898. What are the cost implications?

899. Do strategies and tactics aimed at less than full control reduce the costs of management or simply shift the cost burden?

900. What makes you different or better than others companies selling the same thing?

3.5 Quality Audit: Investment Priorities

901. How does your organization know that its range of activities are being reviewed as rigorously and constructively as they could be?

902. Have the risks associated with the intentions been identified, analyzed and appropriate responses developed?

903. How does your organization know that the quality of its supervisors is appropriately effective and constructive?

904. Does the audit organization have experience in performing the required work for entities of your type and size?

905. Are all areas associated with the storage and reconditioning of devices clean, free of rubbish, adequately ventilated and in good repair?

906. How does your organization know that the research supervision provided to its staff is appropriately effective and constructive?

907. How does your organization know that its research programs are appropriately effective and constructive?

908. How does your organization know that its Governance system is appropriately effective and

constructive?

909. How does your organization know that the support for its staff is appropriately effective and constructive?

910. How does your organization know that its financial management system is appropriately effective and constructive?

911. What are the main things that hinder your ability to do a good job?

912. How does your organization know that the system for managing its facilities is appropriately effective and constructive?

913. Does the report read coherently?

914. How does your organization know that its systems for meeting staff extracurricular learning support requirements are appropriately effective and constructive?

915. Are people allowed to contribute ideas?

916. How does your organization know that its research funding systems are appropriately effective and constructive in enabling quality research outcomes?

917. What experience do staff have in the type of work that the audit entails?

918. How does your organization know that its relationships with the community at large are

appropriately effective and constructive?

919. How does your organization know that it is effectively and constructively guiding staff through to timely completion of tasks?

920. Are adequate and conveniently located toilet facilities available for use by the employees?

3.6 Team Directory: Investment Priorities

921. Process decisions: are contractors adequately prosecuting the work?

922. Process decisions: how well was task order work performed?

923. When will you produce deliverables?

924. Who are the Team Members?

925. Who are your stakeholders (customers, sponsors, end users, team members)?

926. Who will report Investment Priorities project status to all stakeholders?

927. Process decisions: do job conditions warrant additional actions to collect job information and document on-site activity?

928. Process decisions: are there any statutory or regulatory issues relevant to the timely execution of work?

929. Process decisions: do invoice amounts match accepted work in place?

930. Process decisions: which organizational elements and which individuals will be assigned management functions?

931. How do unidentified risks impact the outcome of the Investment Priorities project?

932. Contract requirements complied with?

933. Process decisions: are all start-up, turn over and close out requirements of the contract satisfied?

934. Process decisions: is work progressing on schedule and per contract requirements?

935. What needs to be communicated?

936. Who should receive information (all stakeholders)?

937. Do purchase specifications and configurations match requirements?

938. When does information need to be distributed?

3.7 Team Operating Agreement: Investment Priorities

939. What is the anticipated procedure (recruitment, solicitation of volunteers, or assignment) for selecting team members?

940. What are the boundaries (organizational or geographic) within which you operate?

941. Do you upload presentation materials in advance and test the technology?

942. To whom do you deliver your services?

943. What individual strengths does each team member bring to the group?

944. Methodologies: how will key team processes be implemented, such as training, research, work deliverable production, review and approval processes, knowledge management, and meeting procedures?

945. What are the safety issues/risks that need to be addressed and/or that the team needs to consider?

946. How do you want to be thought of and known within your organization?

947. Must your members collaborate successfully to complete Investment Priorities projects?

948. Did you prepare participants for the next meeting?

949. What are some potential sources of conflict among team members?

950. Do you post any action items, due dates, and responsibilities on the team website?

951. Do you call or email participants to ensure understanding, follow-through and commitment to the meeting outcomes?

952. Do you solicit member feedback about meetings and what would make them better?

953. Did you determine the technology methods that best match the messages to be communicated?

954. Did you draft the meeting agenda?

955. Do you post meeting notes and the recording (if used) and notify participants?

956. Do you determine the meeting length and time of day?

957. What administrative supports will be put in place to support the team and the teams supervisor?

958. Seconds for members to respond?

3.8 Team Performance Assessment: Investment Priorities

959. To what degree does the teams approach to its work allow for modification and improvement over time?

960. When a reviewer complains about method variance, what is the essence of the complaint?

961. How much interpersonal friction is there in your team?

962. To what degree are the relative importance and priority of the goals clear to all team members?

963. To what degree can the team ensure that all members are individually and jointly accountable for the teams purpose, goals, approach, and work-products?

964. Do you give group members authority to make at least some important decisions?

965. To what degree are the goals ambitious?

966. To what degree are fresh input and perspectives systematically caught and added (for example, through information and analysis, new members, and senior sponsors)?

967. How hard did you try to make a good selection?

968. To what degree does the teams purpose constitute a broader, deeper aspiration than just accomplishing short-term goals?

969. What makes opportunities more or less obvious?

970. To what degree are the teams goals and objectives clear, simple, and measurable?

971. Do friends perform better than acquaintances?

972. How do you encourage members to learn from each other?

973. Effects of crew composition on crew performance: Does the whole equal the sum of its parts?

974. To what degree do all members feel responsible for all agreed-upon measures?

975. What is method variance?

976. How hard do you try to make a good selection?

977. Lack of method variance in self-reported affect and perceptions at work: Reality or artifact?

978. To what degree do team members feel that the purpose of the team is important, if not exciting?

3.9 Team Member Performance Assessment: Investment Priorities

979. What resources do you need?

980. To what degree can team members frequently and easily communicate with one another?

981. What does collaboration look like?

982. In what areas would you like to concentrate your knowledge and resources?

983. How do you start collaborating?

984. What, if any, steps are available for employees who feel they have been unfairly or inaccurately rated?

985. What evidence supports your decision-making?

986. What is the target group for instruction (e.g., individual and collective or small team instruction)?

987. To what degree is there a sense that only the team can succeed?

988. What happens if a team member receives a Rating of Unsatisfactory?

989. To what degree are the goals realistic?

990. How will they be formed?

991. How is assessment information achieved, stored?

992. To what degree will new and supplemental skills be introduced as the need is recognized?

993. What changes do you need to make to align practices with beliefs?

994. Does the rater (supervisor) have to wait for the interim or final performance assessment review to tell an employee that the employees performance is unsatisfactory?

995. How effective is training that is delivered through technology-based platforms?

996. What evaluation results did you have?

997. What are best practices in use for the performance measurement system?

998. What were the challenges that resulted for training and assessment?

3.10 Issue Log: Investment Priorities

999. Who reported the issue?

1000. Can you think of other people who might have concerns or interests?

1001. What approaches to you feel are the best ones to use?

1002. What does the stakeholder need from the team?

1003. What are the stakeholders interrelationships?

1004. Why do you manage human resources?

1005. Which stakeholders are thought leaders, influences, or early adopters?

1006. Why multiple evaluators?

1007. What date was the issue resolved?

1008. Is access to the Issue Log controlled?

1009. Are they needed?

1010. Who is involved as you identify stakeholders?

1011. Are stakeholder roles recognized by your organization?

1012. What are the typical contents?

1013. What is a Stakeholder?

1014. How do you reply to this question; you am new here and managing this major program. How do you suggest you build your network?

4.0 Monitoring and Controlling Process Group: Investment Priorities

1015. Did you implement the program as designed?

1016. Have operating capacities been created and/or reinforced in partners?

1017. Did it work?

1018. How was the program set-up initiated?

1019. What areas does the group agree are the biggest success on the Investment Priorities project?

1020. User: who wants the information and what are they interested in?

1021. Is there adequate validation on required fields?

1022. Is there undesirable impact on staff or resources?

1023. Is progress on outcomes due to your program?

1024. Is the schedule for the set products being met?

1025. How to ensure validity, quality and consistency?

1026. How will staff learn how to use the deliverables?

1027. How many more potential communications channels were introduced by the discovery of the new stakeholders?

1028. How is agile Investment Priorities project management done?

1029. How well defined and documented were the Investment Priorities project management processes you chose to use?

1030. Who are the Investment Priorities project stakeholders?

1031. In what way has the program come up with innovative measures for problem-solving?

1032. How are you doing?

4.1 Project Performance Report: Investment Priorities

1033. To what degree do the relationships of the informal organization motivate taskrelevant behavior and facilitate task completion?

1034. To what degree do team members articulate the teams work approach?

1035. To what degree does the teams work approach provide opportunity for members to engage in results-based evaluation?

1036. To what degree do the goals specify concrete team work products?

1037. To what degree does the information network provide individuals with the information they require?

1038. To what degree does the task meet individual needs?

1039. To what degree does the information network communicate information relevant to the task?

1040. To what degree can the cognitive capacity of individuals accommodate the flow of information?

1041. To what degree do the structures of the formal organization motivate taskrelevant behavior and facilitate task completion?

1042. To what degree are the demands of the task compatible with and converge with the relationships of the informal organization?

1043. To what degree do members articulate the goals beyond the team membership?

1044. To what degree is there centralized control of information sharing?

1045. To what degree can team members meet frequently enough to accomplish the teams ends?

1046. To what degree are the structures of the formal organization consistent with the behaviors in the informal organization?

1047. To what degree do team members frequently explore the teams purpose and its implications?

1048. To what degree does the teams purpose contain themes that are particularly meaningful and memorable?

4.2 Variance Analysis: Investment Priorities

1049. Are overhead cost budgets established for each department which has authority to incur overhead costs?

1050. What is the dollar amount of the fluctuation?

1051. Can process improvements lead to unfavorable variances?

1052. How do you identify and isolate causes of favorable and unfavorable cost and schedule variances?

1053. How do you identify potential or actual overruns and underruns?

1054. What should management do?

1055. How does your organization measure performance?

1056. Is the anticipated (firm and potential) business base Investment Priorities projected in a rational, consistent manner?

1057. How have the setting and use of standards changed over time?

1058. Who is generally responsible for monitoring and taking action on variances?

1059. How do you verify authorization to proceed with all authorized work?

1060. What causes selling price variance?

1061. Why are standard cost systems used?

1062. Are material costs reported within the same period as that in which BCWP is earned for that material?

1063. How are variances affected by multiple material and labor categories?

1064. Did a new competitor enter the market?

1065. Are overhead costs budgets established on a basis consistent with the anticipated direct business base?

1066. What is the total budget for the Investment Priorities project (including estimates for authorized and unpriced work)?

1067. What is the budgeted cost for work scheduled?

1068. Contemplated overhead expenditure for each period based on the best information currently is available?

4.3 Earned Value Status: Investment Priorities

1069. How does this compare with other Investment Priorities projects?

1070. When is it going to finish?

1071. Verification is a process of ensuring that the developed system satisfies the stakeholders agreements and specifications; Are you building the product right? What do you verify?

1072. Where are your problem areas?

1073. If earned value management (EVM) is so good in determining the true status of a Investment Priorities project and Investment Priorities project its completion, why is it that hardly any one uses it in information systems related Investment Priorities projects?

1074. Validation is a process of ensuring that the developed system will actually achieve the stakeholders desired outcomes; Are you building the right product? What do you validate?

1075. What is the unit of forecast value?

1076. Where is evidence-based earned value in your organization reported?

1077. How much is it going to cost by the finish?

1078. Are you hitting your Investment Priorities projects targets?

1079. Earned value can be used in almost any Investment Priorities project situation and in almost any Investment Priorities project environment. it may be used on large Investment Priorities projects, medium sized Investment Priorities projects, tiny Investment Priorities projects (in cut-down form), complex and simple Investment Priorities projects and in any market sector. some people, of course, know all about earned value, they have used it for years - but perhaps not as effectively as they could have?

4.4 Risk Audit: Investment Priorities

1080. Does willful intent modify risk-based auditing?

1081. What responsibilities for quality, errors, and outcomes have been delegated to staff (or others) without adequate oversight?

1082. Do you have financial policies and procedures in place to guide officers of your organization/treasurer/ general members?

1083. What is happening in other jurisdictions? Could that happen here?

1084. What compliance systems do you have in place to address quality, errors, and outcomes?

1085. Do you meet the legislative requirements (for example PAYG, super contributions) for paid employees?

1086. What are the benefits of a Enterprise wide approach to Risk Management?

1087. How do you govern assets?

1088. Are there any forms the staff is required to sign?

1089. What effect would a better risk management program have had?

1090. Have risks been considered with an insurance broker or provider and suitable insurance cover been arranged?

1091. How do you manage risk?

1092. Are enough people available?

1093. Will participants be required to sign a legally counselled waiver or risk disclaimer when entering an event?

1094. Is your organization willing to commit significant time to the requirements gathering process?

1095. Are you willing to seek legal advice when required?

1096. Is all expenditure authorised through an identified process?

4.5 Contractor Status Report: Investment Priorities

1097. If applicable; describe your standard schedule for new software version releases. Are new software version releases included in the standard maintenance plan?

1098. What are the minimum and optimal bandwidth requirements for the proposed solution?

1099. How is risk transferred?

1100. What process manages the contracts?

1101. What was the actual budget or estimated cost for your organizations services?

1102. What was the final actual cost?

1103. How long have you been using the services?

1104. What was the budget or estimated cost for your organizations services?

1105. Describe how often regular updates are made to the proposed solution. Are corresponding regular updates included in the standard maintenance plan?

1106. How does the proposed individual meet each requirement?

1107. What was the overall budget or estimated cost?

1108. Are there contractual transfer concerns?

1109. What is the average response time for answering a support call?

1110. Who can list a Investment Priorities project as organization experience, your organization or a previous employee of your organization?

4.6 Formal Acceptance: Investment Priorities

1111. How well did the team follow the methodology?

1112. How does your team plan to obtain formal acceptance on your Investment Priorities project?

1113. Who supplies data?

1114. Do you buy-in installation services?

1115. Do you perform formal acceptance or burn-in tests?

1116. Does it do what Investment Priorities project team said it would?

1117. Was business value realized?

1118. Have all comments been addressed?

1119. Is formal acceptance of the Investment Priorities project product documented and distributed?

1120. Was the Investment Priorities project work done on time, within budget, and according to specification?

1121. Do you buy pre-configured systems or build your own configuration?

1122. Who would use it?

1123. Was the sponsor/customer satisfied?

1124. What is the Acceptance Management Process?

1125. Was the client satisfied with the Investment Priorities project results?

1126. What are the requirements against which to test, Who will execute?

1127. What function(s) does it fill or meet?

1128. Was the Investment Priorities project goal achieved?

1129. Does it do what client said it would?

1130. Did the Investment Priorities project achieve its MOV?

5.0 Closing Process Group: Investment Priorities

1131. Are there funding or time constraints?

1132. What business situation is being addressed?

1133. Based on your Investment Priorities project communication management plan, what worked well?

1134. What level of risk does the proposed budget represent to the Investment Priorities project?

1135. Did you do what you said you were going to do?

1136. Who are the Investment Priorities project stakeholders?

1137. What is the amount of funding and what Investment Priorities project phases are funded?

1138. How critical is the Investment Priorities project success to the success of your organization?

1139. Does the close educate others to improve performance?

1140. Is this an updated Investment Priorities project Proposal Document?

1141. What could have been improved?

1142. What were things that you did very well and want to do the same again on the next Investment Priorities project?

1143. Did the Investment Priorities project management methodology work?

1144. What were the actual outcomes?

1145. What areas does the group agree are the biggest success on the Investment Priorities project?

1146. What areas were overlooked on this Investment Priorities project?

1147. Did the Investment Priorities project team have enough people to execute the Investment Priorities project plan?

1148. How well did the team follow the chosen processes?

1149. Did you do things well?

5.1 Procurement Audit: Investment Priorities

1150. How do you confirm whether the contracted organization supplied the goods or executed the work as per the quality, quantity and price indicated in the contract agreement/ supply order?

1151. Are there authorizations on file to support all deductions from payroll checks?

1152. In the set up of the system and in the award of contracts were only electronic means used?

1153. Is there no evidence of any individual on the evaluation panel being biased?

1154. Is there a practice that prohibits signing blank purchase orders?

1155. Relevance of the contract to the Internal Market?

1156. Does the individual approving disbursements sign or initial the document?

1157. Are rules in automatic disbursement programs adequate to prevent duplicate payment of invoices?

1158. Does the procurement process compile basic procurement information such as how much is bought and spend with individual suppliers?

1159. Has an upper limit of cost been fixed?

1160. Were additional deliveries a partial replacement for normal supplies or installations or an extension of existing supplies or installations?

1161. Are there procedures governing how sales and use tax will be handled (ordering in state versus ordering out of state)?

1162. Are internal control systems in place?

1163. Are all purchase orders accounted for?

1164. Is there a policy on making purchases locally where possible?

1165. How do you ensure whether the goods were supplied or works executed in time and properly recorded in measurement books and stock/works registers after inspection?

1166. Are all mutilated and voided checks retained for proper accounting of pre-numbered checks?

1167. If an electronic auction or a dynamic purchasing system was used, did the tender documents specify details on access to information, electronic equipment used and connection specifications?

1168. Are there internal control systems in place to secure that laws and regulations are observed?

1169. Do appropriate controls ensure that procurement decisions are not biased by conflicts of interest or corruption?

5.2 Contract Close-Out: Investment Priorities

1170. Why Outsource?

1171. Has each contract been audited to verify acceptance and delivery?

1172. What is capture management?

1173. Change in circumstances?

1174. Have all contracts been closed?

1175. Have all acceptance criteria been met prior to final payment to contractors?

1176. How is the contracting office notified of the automatic contract close-out?

1177. Was the contract sufficiently clear so as not to result in numerous disputes and misunderstandings?

1178. Parties: Authorized?

1179. Was the contract complete without requiring numerous changes and revisions?

1180. Was the contract type appropriate?

1181. Have all contracts been completed?

1182. Parties: who is involved?

1183. Change in attitude or behavior?

1184. How does it work?

1185. What happens to the recipient of services?

1186. Are the signers the authorized officials?

1187. Have all contract records been included in the Investment Priorities project archives?

1188. How/when used ?

1189. Change in knowledge?

5.3 Project or Phase Close-Out: Investment Priorities

1190. Does the lesson educate others to improve performance?

1191. What information is each stakeholder group interested in?

1192. Which changes might a stakeholder be required to make as a result of the Investment Priorities project?

1193. In addition to assessing whether the Investment Priorities project was successful, it is equally critical to analyze why it was or was not fully successful. Are you including this?

1194. What was expected from each stakeholder?

1195. Were risks identified and mitigated?

1196. In preparing the Lessons Learned report, should it reflect a consensus viewpoint, or should the report reflect the different individual viewpoints?

1197. What is in it for you?

1198. How much influence did the stakeholder have over others?

1199. What was learned?

1200. What can you do better next time, and what specific actions can you take to improve?

1201. What security considerations needed to be addressed during the procurement life cycle?

1202. Planned completion date?

1203. What benefits or impacts does the stakeholder group expect to obtain as a result of the Investment Priorities project?

1204. What are the marketing communication needs for each stakeholder?

1205. What was the preferred delivery mechanism?

1206. What are the informational communication needs for each stakeholder?

1207. What are the mandatory communication needs for each stakeholder?

1208. Did the Investment Priorities project management methodology work?

5.4 Lessons Learned: Investment Priorities

1209. What Investment Priorities project circumstances were not anticipated?

1210. How well did the scope of the Investment Priorities project match what was defined in the Investment Priorities project Proposal?

1211. Would you spend your own time fixing this issue?

1212. Recommendation: what do you recommend should be done to ensure that others throughout your organization can benefit from what you have learned?

1213. What report generation capability is needed?

1214. What on the Investment Priorities project worked well and was effective in the delivery of the product?

1215. Who needs to learn lessons?

1216. What did you put in place to ensure success?

1217. Under what legal authority did your organization head and program manager direct your organization and Investment Priorities project?

1218. Was there a Investment Priorities project

Definition document. Was there a Investment Priorities project Plan. Were they used during the Investment Priorities project?

1219. What is the proportion of in-house and contractor personnel authorized for the Investment Priorities project?

1220. What if anything has been lacking?

1221. Can the lesson learned be replicated?

1222. Were all interests adequately involved/ informed?

1223. Was the necessary hardware, software, accommodation etc available?

1224. Did the Investment Priorities project improve the team members reputations, skills, personal development?

1225. How effective was Investment Priorities project Team member training?

1226. What are the internal fiscal constraints?

1227. How closely did deliverables match what was defined within the Investment Priorities project Scope?

1228. How clearly defined were the objectives for this Investment Priorities project?

Index

264

manages   76, 82, 129, 248
managing   2, 85, 125, 127, 130, 203, 226, 237
Mandated   203
mandatory   222, 259
manner   17, 86, 127, 152-153, 220, 242
mantle 123
mapping   63-64, 69, 215
market 19, 131, 243, 245, 254
marketer   7
marketing   110, 142, 259
markets   22
Maslow   170
Master 174
material   153, 243
materials   1, 230
matrices   144
Matrix 2-5, 131, 144, 185, 189-190, 203
matter 31, 45, 52
matters   224
maximizing   119
McClellan   170
McGregor   170
meaningful   44, 119, 190, 241
measurable   27, 39, 152, 215, 233
measure   2, 9, 17, 28, 42-44, 49, 52-53, 55-56, 61, 74, 77, 80-
81, 84, 92-93, 95, 128, 179, 182, 185, 242
measured   48-49, 54-56, 94, 99, 185, 205
measures   44-47, 49, 51, 54, 64, 69, 71, 78, 91, 97, 133, 184-
185, 233, 239
measuring   190
mechanical   1
mechanics   219
mechanism   149, 203, 259
mechanisms   43, 46, 131
mechanized   155
medium   245
meeting   31, 33, 100, 138-139, 156, 187, 196, 208, 218, 223,
226, 230-231
meetings   34, 38, 139-140, 146, 176, 208, 215, 223, 231
megatrends   117
member   5, 33, 112, 121, 195, 217, 230-231, 234, 261
members   29, 38, 72, 91, 133, 140, 155, 173, 175, 191, 195-
196, 212, 228, 230-234, 240-241, 246, 261

287

CPSIA information can be obtained
at www.ICGtesting.com
Printed in the USA
BVHW041010200819
556236BV00011B/699/P